THEY *Tore Down* THE
RUSSELL HOTEL

A Story of Change in Small Town Mexico

To Shirley
Hope you enjoy
the book.
Joe Easby

By

DAVE EASBY

ISBN: 1452856397
ISBN-13: 9781452856391

TABLE OF CONTENTS

THANKS

I owe a debt of gratitude to a number of people who helped in making this book become a reality. The members of the Dunedin Florida Writers Group offered both encouragement and positive criticism that helped, in the end, make this a better product. I certainly appreciate the keen eye of Beth Fillier, who reviewed the final product for me, and Johan Nielsen was a great asset in reviewing the first draft. My thanks also go to Barb and Hugh Elliott, Pat Valliere and Bob and Rita Laroche who read a fictional version I had done earlier, before I realized that there was enough humour and life in the true stories of our time in Jaltemba Bay that there was no need to muddy them up with drug dealers and crooked cops. The folks at CreateSpace were great to work with. My wife Anne served as both my co-pilot and soul mate in these adventures and also provided honest and sometimes humbling feedback. But the biggest thanks of all must go to the folks of Jaltemba Bay — permanent and seasonal residents alike — who welcomed us into their little corner of paradise.

The stories in this book are largely true and, where I have taken some literary license, it is likely in the places where you would least suspect it. Truth is, in fact, stranger than fiction. The names have been changed to protect the innocent. And, sometimes, the not so innocent.

INTRODUCTION

I have known the Russell Hotel only as a falling-down shell of a building that sat at the north end of Circuito Libertad. It's the street that runs along the beach; the street that some day will run parallel to the malecon, the one that they finalized the plans for in 1999. I have known it only as a place where homeless sought shelter and where only the bravest would go when Los Amigos de La Peñita did their first annual beach clean-up.

The Russell had ceased operating long before my wife Anne and I first came to La Peñita de Jaltemba, a small Mexican town that sits along the Pacific coast, a little over an hour north of Puerto Vallarta by Pacifico bus. I have never met a Mr. Russell or a Mrs. Russell or even a Señor Russell, if there ever were any such people, and I have yet to meet someone who has. At least one of the old-timers has told me that it was never more than 'accommodation of last resort'.

It was in 2007 in our fourth winter in La Peñita when we saw the headline in the Jaltemba Sol, the online newspaper that bills itself as "the heartbeat of Riviera Nayarit". They were tearing down the Russell Hotel. I watched the trucks full of rubble and dust rumble past our apartment. I even followed one, just to make sure they weren't dumping it in the estuary that runs just to the south – not that I would have known what to do if they were.

The demolition, in the logic of Mexico, meant a beginning rather than an end. There are many abandoned buildings here. They sit and fall and lean precariously along the beach. Demolition costs money and one does not invest money unless one intends to build something in its place.

Rumours flew that winter. In the bars. At the market. On Jaltemba Bay Folk – the local internet bulletin board. The Decamaron, which already ran the largest all-inclusive resort in these parts, was building a resort here. The Sheraton had bought the property. Two brothers from Idaho were going to put in a bed and breakfast. Bill Gates, who's Chief Financial Officer's first cousin's college roommate's ex-boyfriend had spent last winter here, was going to build a retreat.

La Peñita was once a small fishing and farming town, but it now lies at the heart of Riviera Nayarit: the new tourist destination that the Mexican Government is working hard to promote. Nothing symbolized the transformation more than the demolition of the Russell Hotel.

But you see signs of it everywhere.

Like a water truck standing diagonally across the intersection, two massive tree trunks holding it up where the rear wheels have fallen off, the driver sitting patiently on the curb. He is in no hurry. Business is off since the town raised enough money from the influx of folks from up north to get their well fixed. Now water actually flows through the maze of dusty pipes which crisscross under the cobblestone streets.

Or the young mother, sixteen at best, smiling broadly as she pushes the wheelbarrow up the street. Her child sleeps soundly in its tray where there had once been a mound of raw oysters, as she wheels it past a young man hawking souvenir T-shirts. The shirts are all adorned with turtles and whales and palm trees. They are mostly emblazoned with Puerto Vallarta but the occasional local one has begun to make its way into his inventory.

Or the donkey standing stoically in the back of his pick-up truck. His nose twitches at the unfamiliar sweet scent of basil and oregano that drifts by from the cozy new Italian restaurant across the street.

There are three towns that make up the community of Jaltemba Bay. Rincon de Guayabitos is the quintessential Mexican beach town: hotels and bungalows that sit half-occupied most of the year but are crammed at Christmas and Easter with Mexican families who flock to the sea from Tepic and Guadalajara.. There's a residential section of million dollar homes that is sometimes referred to as 'Gringo Gulch.' Los Ayala, to the south, is a smaller version of Guayabitos – minus the millionaire homes. And then there is La Peñita to the north. It's a working town; home to the locals who work in the hotels and restaurants and stores of Guayabitos. But, even here, Nord Americano condos have begun the steady creep up from the south.

Jaltemba Bay draws few foreign short-term visitors, although the numbers have been inching higher, but a tightly-knit community of Canadians and Americans make it their winter home. Most have been coming here for years. They gather every Thursday for rib night at Mateja's on the beach. They come out for the horseshoe tournament to raise money for scholarships for local students. They help teach English in the schools. And when a long-term resident was killed in an accident, they drew eight hundred people to a benefit concert to pay the expenses of his widow.

There is much talk among the Nord Americano community about how long the 'Canadian Condos', at three stories, will remain the tallest building in La Peñita. About how long it will be before the Carlos and Charlie's restaurant chain opens a branch here and a Walmart puts all the wonderful little supermercados out of business. And about when the new airport will be built in Las Varas, just up the highway, to accommodate jumbo jets full of tourists.

But for now it remains in limbo. Half old. Half new. A town in transition. A town with stories to tell.

1.
WHY A BEE TOES

We still have the deck of cards, the one that has "Guayabitos" printed ever so carefully on the inside flap of the box; we wanted to make sure we had the spelling right.

It was our back-up plan; something we could show the bus driver if he couldn't comprehend our mangled attempts to pronounce the name of the town that our new friend Marlene had told us about.

"Why a bee toes, Why a bee toes," we repeated, sounding out each syllable as we followed her lead.

We knew that getting it wrong might mean getting dumped off the bus in the middle of nowhere. Sure, we had the cards as Plan B, but that seemed so lame. We knew we could do it. But then, this was to be our first big foray out into rural Mexico.

Paco, in his starched shirt and black bowtie, waited patiently as I signed off the bill for the four Piña Coladas. I wondered how he could stand there in the grueling January afternoon sun in a long sleeve shirt and long pants; I'm sure he was equally curious as to why I wasn't freezing to death in nothing but a swimsuit.

We were sitting around the pool at the Sheraton Buganvilias Vacation Club in Puerto Vallarta: Anne, me and our new friends, Marlene and Doug. It was remarkably quiet for the number of people, or at least the number of towels, hanging around the pool. We knew from experience, that many of the loungers that had a towel or a paperback or both sitting on them as an 'occupied' sign would be vacant most of the day. Their owners were either at the beach or back in their rooms or even downtown. The towels appeared early every morning, dropped off as people made their way to the restaurant for breakfast.

The soft background music was interrupted only by the soft idle chatter of guests and shouts of "Bingo, Bingo" from the activity director at the hotel next door. There were few children to laugh and splash in the water at this time of year. And, other than Paco and his co-workers, even fewer Mexicans.

"It's about an hour and a half on the bus," Marlene continued. "You have to catch the Pacifico Bus at the terminal downtown."

"You can take either the Guadalajara or the Tepic bus," added Doug. "They will both stop there, but you have to let the driver know as there isn't a terminal in Guayabitos."

"It's easy," Marlene noted in response to our 'deer in the headlights' expressions. "And you will love the place. It's very quiet and the beach is gorgeous."

Marlene and Doug were fellow Canadians. They had been coming to Mexico for ten years now.

"We like to get out of the cities," Doug said. "See some real Mexico. There are great little towns all the way up the coast."

This was the fourth trip to this country for me and my wife Anne. But we knew this was not all that Mexico had to offer and we were anxious to see the parts of Mexico that lay beyond the crowded beaches and glittering resorts and chain restaurants.

Our first Mexican destination had been Cancun; the brochures had certainly made it seem clean and safe enough. It was that. But we soon found that it wasn't Mexico; it was just Miami with better weather and cheaper prices. It was all hotels and malls and restaurants: a cement city bordering the ocean that was cut out of the jungle. We never found the part of town where the locals live, if there is one. Maybe they bus everyone in from the outlying villages.

We did venture out once, on an organized tour to Chichen Itza. Chichen Itza is an archaeological site that dates back to the heyday of the Maya civilization. The ruins are magnificent: the step pyramid that is El Castillo, the Temple of the Warriors and the Great Ballcourt. The last of these was the most impressive.

"166 by 68 meters, with 12 meter high walls," the guide explained. "It was the scene of ancient Mesoamerican ballgames."

A sculptured panel on one of the walls featured a player who had been decapitated.

"The price of a 'bad game' was significantly higher in those days," Anne had said.

"Yeah, today, it might just mean a pay cut from ten million a year to eight."

But it was another tour stop that stays with me, an unscheduled one. It was a little hole-in-the-wall town along the way: a dozen shanties, a supermercado and a pharmacia. We watched a young woman nervously whisper something to the tour guide. We saw forty puzzled looks as the bus screeched to a halt. Forty pairs of eyes watched her exit the bus with the guide and enter the pharmacia; there was no door, just wide metal gates. Forty necks craned to see her point to the top shelf and the clerk scamper up the ladder to fetch the object of her attention; there is no self serve here. Forty mouths snickered as she returned to the bus, sanitary pads in hand. This is not a place for the shy.

We chose a more secluded community for our second trip to Mexico: Melaque, a smaller town about an hour from the city of Manzanillo. It was all-inclusive so there was no need to go anywhere and no way to get there even if we wanted to.

My most vivid memory, for some reason is: 'Thus Spake Zarathustra', the opening theme from 2001: A Space Odyssey. Every night at five, it would echo through the grounds of the resort, loud and booming. We watched the guests rise from their chairs or exit their rooms or march up from the beach. Eyes glazed over. Drawn to the resort dining room like lemmings by the haunting melody. We even made a home video of it called 'Night of the Living Buffet Eaters.' We watch it, well, actually, never. It's stored with all other photos and videos and odds and ends that we've accumulated from years of travel.

Thus Spake Zarathustra was our signal to head the other way, to Barra de Navidad: the one place we could walk to. It was down a long stretch of mostly deserted beach. It had the most beautiful sunsets in the world and a dilapidated little bar that served Corona with a half lime squeezed into the neck. It was where we would celebrate the end of another day of doing nothing.

And it had something else: a small collection of American expats who, like us, spent every sunset at Fred's Place. They were a motley crew who had clearly enjoyed the sixties much more than anyone had a right to. The sickly sweet smell of forbidden pleasure wafted up from the large table they had claimed for themselves. The Corona flowed; they had been here long before our resort had begun to crank up the stereo for the buffet call. There was Danny and Stretch, Missy and Kat. Fred knew every name. It was clear that they were not 'two-weekers'; they were here for the long haul.

It was as we watched and listened, that the notion of spending a winter in Mexico some day began to take shape.

Third time's a charm. Puerto Vallarta was the third place we hit in Mexico and it had it all: a fine sand beach, lots of restaurants, great hotels and a downtown with real old Mexican charm – and real Mexicans. It was not an uneventful visit.

On the second day, the palapa restaurant next to the pool caught fire. We watched from our twelfth floor balcony as the flames soared high above our head. The air was thick and black. The heat was intense. And the one poor waiter who was left on duty scooped up bucket after bucket of water from the pool and dumped them helplessly on the raging inferno. It was two hours later when the "Bomberos" arrived to provide him some relief, driving a fire engine that looked like it came straight out of an episode of 'Leave It To Beaver.' By then, the fire had burned itself out.

On the fourth day, after they moved us next door, we were robbed. It was only a few dollars and we knew the culprit: the young man refilling our servi-bar. I still have a copy of the police report. Actually, it's the original; the head of security gave it back to me on our last day. Case closed.

It was two days later; our taxi driver regaled us with Frank Sinatra tunes, the words butchered beyond all recognition, as he raced through the busy streets like Mario Andretti. And when he missed the back end of a city bus by the slimmest of margins, we decided that, with all this good luck, this was the place we wanted to invest. We bought a timeshare.

"Do you have an inbitation?"

They are the words all visitors to Puerto Vallarta dread. The timeshare merchants are everywhere. They pose as waiters and tourist guides and tequila sellers. They lurk in restaurants and gift shops. Even the EcoTours store which looks like it comes out of the pages of the National Geographic is a timeshare front. They offer cash or discounts or other trinkets to attend a presentation where they proffer a huge array of options: fixed weeks, floating weeks, points, prime weeks, floating super prime weeks, floating super prime every other year weeks. If it had been 1999, I'm sure they would have offered floating super prime every other millennium weeks.

As newbies, we were no match for them. A 'free breakfast', four hours and a couple of margaritas later, we were the proud owners of Unit 1502, Week 50 at the Sheraton Buganvilias Vacation Club.

So here we sat the following year, back at the Sheraton Buganvilias Vacation Club, drinking Piña Coladas around the pool and talking to our new friends Marlene and Doug about this charming little town called Guayabitos that they had visited last year. We were anxious to see more of this beautiful country.

It was eight the next morning when we caught the Pacifico Bus: the one that said Tepic on the front. It was a second class bus but that was still a big jump up from the rattletraps that masqueraded as city buses.

I had my deck of playing cards in my pocket but I was determined to take my best shot.

"Why a bee toes?" I asked, slowly and concisely.

The driver nodded and motioned to us to get on.

I must confess that I don't remember much of the trip. I think I was too preoccupied with making sure that we didn't miss our stop. I recall a highway that wound its way up and down the mountains, past pineapple farms and sickly looking cattle and dried-up river beds. I remember passing through or past a number of towns and checking each one carefully against the name printed on the inside of our card box.

The driver called the name out loudly and waited to make sure we got off before he headed off on his way

There was not much to see in Guayabitos. There was a main street with a series of restaurants and small shops selling beach toys and cheap jewelry. There was a butcher shop and a couple of supermercados. There was a street to the west that ran parallel to the beach with a series of small family bungalows and hotels. It was quaint and cute and quiet. It was very quiet.

The beach was magnificent. It was a gorgeous expanse of white sand with a slow gentle slope out into the ocean. And it was empty.

We wandered the streets and meandered through the shops. We sat on the beach and watched the gentle waves roll in. We ate shrimp tacos at Salvador's and stared into the vast ocean.

I'm not sure exactly what the big attraction was. Maybe it was the stark contrast between this sleepy little town and the hustle and bustle that was Puerto Vallarta. It was dark when the Pacifico bus swept its way into town but the bright lights from the hotels and bars and restaurants reflected off the black pavement. The streets were packed with cars and pedestrians. Blaring music called out to potential patrons.

We were still ten years away from retirement, but we both knew it as the bus pulled into the terminal downtown: Guayabitos would be our home for the first winter of that particular part of our lives.

"Why a bee toes," Anne intoned with a smile. "I guess I better learn to say it right."

2.

DARK ROADS AND NICE ASSES

"This is where we live," Laura said proudly.

Anne and I stared out the window looking for any signs of life, and saw nothing but blackness and a small break in the vegetation where a road could possibly be. And we began to get nervous.

It had been ten years since we had made that trip on the Pacifico Bus to Guayabitos. But that had been in the daylight and things looked entirely different at night. The narrow band of asphalt that wound its way up and down the mountains had provided splendid views in the bright morning sun. Now, the darkness was punctuated only by the bright headlights of the odd vehicle careening down the mountains toward us and the dim lights of an occasional town. Well, actually, there were no real towns per se, just signs that promised that there were indeed towns and villages and hamlets just off the road.

"Ursula Galvan," Laura added reassuringly. But we were anything but reassured.

Laura was the other half of Laura and Kenny. She was from a small town just down the coast; he was from Canada.

"I have lived down here for fifteen years," Kenny had written in one of his emails. "Back then I was pretty much the only gringo in town."

We had never actually talked to Kenny. We had found the apartment on the internet. We were not particularly demanding in our needs: two bedrooms, close to the beach, a balcony, English language TV - it would after all be for six months – and cheap. Our negotiations had all been through email. For all we knew, 'Kenny' might be, in reality, Harriet – a sixty year old widow in Dublin, Ohio who had never even been to Mexico, did not own property there and was laughing, literally, all the way to the bank when our deposit money appeared in her account.

We didn't even know there was a Laura until we disembarked from our flight in Puerto Vallarta and saw her standing there holding a piece of paper with 'Easbys' carefully printed out in large letters. I'm not sure who was more relieved. Laura had been waiting patiently for several hours due to the late arrival of our flight and must have been wondering if there were in fact such things as 'Easbys'. Anne and I, on the other hand, now knew that there was a real 'Kenny' and, hopefully, an apartment in Guayabitos waiting for us.

There is a traffic light in Customs at Puerto Vallarta Airport. After retrieving your bags, every family takes their turn at it. Green means you are free to go. Red means you are subject to search which, given the pace of the Mexican bureaucracy, can cause you to spend a sizeable chunk of your holiday in the airport. It turned out to be our lucky day and we gratefully wheeled our three gigantic suitcases out to Laura's car. Suitcases, it turned out, that contained all the stuff we were worried about finding but that was readily available at the local market at half the price, and none of the stuff we would want but couldn't find for the next six months.

The lights were bright and the highway was busy as we passed through the bustling cities of Nuevo Vallarta and Mezcales and Bucerias. It was even busier than I remembered. Anne sat in the front of the dusty green Plymouth with Laura; I sat in the back, sharing the seat with the largest of our bags, two backpacks, a camera, our documents, and a copy of the Toronto Globe and Mail that I had rescued from the flight. I feared it would be the last English language newspaper I would see for the next six months.

The darkness had come about half and hour back, as we passed the turnoff to Punta de Mita on the outskirts of Bucerias. And now, as I peered out into the darkness looking for any signs of Laura and Kenny's home town of Ursula Galvan, the questions raced through my head. Twenty-five years of marriage told me that the same ones haunted Anne; her next words confirmed it.

"The place where we are staying is in Guayabitos though, isn't it?"

I imagined Anne picturing the top of the box of cards and carefully sounding out each syllable.

Maybe there was a place called 'Guayabilos', I thought to myself. A little hole-in-the-wall town with a dozen shanties, a supermercado and a pharmacia like the one we had stopped at many years ago on the way to Chichen Itza for that unfortunate young woman in need of 'supplies'. Maybe I spelled it wrong when I googled it.

"No, No," Laura replied, "Es right in Guayabitos."

"Minutes from the beach?" Anne added. It was part question and part plea.

But Anne and I both knew that the 'minutes from the beach' that had excited us in their ad might just be real estate talk like 'Handyman's Special', and meant minutes from the beach in a car. In a car driven by a Mexican taxi driver. We could be twenty kilometers from town and this description could still apply.

"Yes, very close," Laura assured us.

Had Hurricane Kena, the one that had stripped our timeshare at the Sheraton Buganvilias of its beach, destroyed the wonderful little town of Guayabitos that we had visited ten years ago? Maybe that's why there was no-one on this highway: because there was no place worth visiting in this direction.

I thought back to Anne's words when we had sent off our deposit: "I hope looking for 'cheap' isn't a mistake?"

Our collective sigh of relief must have been audible at a distance as the lights of Guayabitos came into view. The highway went to four lanes and there were three traffic lights. It was a little bigger and busier than we remembered. But other than that, it looked just like the place we had visited ten years before.

Our new home was a four unit building two blocks back from the main street. You could, in fact, only go three blocks back from the main street before you hit the highway to Los Ayala. It was two stories high with a high cement wall surrounding the entire building.

Laura unlocked the wrought iron gates and ushered us into the courtyard, which would also serve as our downstairs neighbour's patio and parking spot. She motioned to the stairs. While we cursed our assignment to the second floor as we hauled our luggage up the stairs, we later learned the benefits of the top level. While a gentle breeze provided some relief for us on those scorching hot afternoons, the outer wall blocked any such respite on the lower patio and our neighbour could roast marshmallows off his bare chest.

We paid Laura the balance of our rent for the season and as she bade us good night and promised that Kenny would come by in the morning, we went through the list of what we had asked for in our internet query.

Two bedrooms. Check.

The apartment was clean but spartan. The main room served as kitchen, dining room and living room and there were indeed two good sized bedrooms and a bathroom that was certainly functional but hardly fancy. The furniture was dark and sturdy – like the old pieces I remember seeing in those Pancho Villa movies.

We could accommodate six of our friends with the four double beds Kenny had supplied, as long as they were very good friends. We could also accommodate the entire population of a small Mexican village if what we had heard was true about how tightly they packed in the locals during Christmas Week or Semana Santa and Semana Pasqua, the two weeks that surround Easter Sunday, when the entire country seems to take a break.

The place was certainly bright, reminding me of one of those cute little Acadian fishing villages that they put on all the post cards. The living room was green, orange and yellow. The bedrooms were green, orange and white. Every wall was two-toned. We found out later that, because all of the buildings here are cement, in order to install plumbing or electrical work, you need to chisel out a channel for the wires or pipes and then cement them back in when they're done. For some reason, when Kenny had filled them in, he used a different shade of paint so you can trace all the wiring and plumbing on the walls. We weren't sure if he did it to facilitate future repairs or because the local paint store couldn't match up the old colours. Or maybe there had just been a sale.

Balcony. Check.

There was a decent size balcony with a palm tree overlooking it to provide some shade and, we were assured, a cool breeze that flowed past it in the afternoon. It had a nice view of the street and the mountains beyond.

It was a view, we later discovered, that provided a great source of entertainment, particularly for Anne. She had become quite infatuated with the Mexican cowboy with the nice ass that rode to work every morning through the vacant lot next door. And then one afternoon, we were sitting on our balcony when we heard a large commotion coming from down the street. All of a sudden, Anne's Mexican cowboy – riding his good-looking ass - rounded the corner leading a cattle drive through the streets of Guayabitos.

Close to the beach. Check.

It was 700 steps; we counted the next day.

English language TV. Check, although a quick scan revealed that Kenny's satellite service featured only an odd selection of specialty channels like the Food Network (The History of Fried Chicken), the Health Network (The World's Most Famous Tumors), the NASA network (video of old shuttle launches) and the Bible Network. We also got Fox News and one night they had Paul Hellyer, who was billed as former Canadian Defense Minister, talking about why he believes in UFOs and aliens from outer space. I packed my 'Proud to be Canadian' T-shirt away for a week after that.

"It could have been worse," I told Anne. "Remember the year we went to Spain and got one station in English."

"Yeah," she replied, "the BBC channel with all the game shows. Remember the one where people got to pick their own categories and chose things like 'The History of Ice Dancing' and who was it?

It was hard to forget.

"Status Quo. Remember their one hit - Pictures of Matchstick Men. And how about that trivia challenge between a team from the Privy Council Office and three representatives from the Romantic Novelists Association."

Even John Cleese couldn't make up stuff like that.

But at least we would have TV and, a few weeks later, Canadian TV at that.

Cheap.

At $650 a month, it was all that we could have hoped for, even if we did have at least one gecko for a roommate and a family of iguanas living in the abandoned pipes in the vacant lot next door.

But, above all, it felt cozy and comfortable. It felt like home.

It was close to midnight by the time we had unpacked and flipped a coin to decide which of us would get two drawers and who would get one in the single dresser we had at our disposal. We had relocated one of the double beds from our room to the 'guest bedroom' which had now become one giant fourteen by six foot mattress with a small walkway on either side. It looked like we were preparing for a Roman orgy. It would do for tonight.

It had been a long day. We had had an early flight and a transfer in Mexico City. We had been convinced that our luggage would be stuck in Mexico City so we had asked everyone who would listen whether we had to retrieve our luggage and go through customs: the flight attendant, the check-in person, the official from Immigration, even the guy cleaning the washrooms. They had all said no but we were nonetheless relieved when we had seen it tumbling down the carousel at Puerto Vallarta airport.

But we had waited a long time for this day and neither of us was ready to hit the sack without a least a quick trip down to the main street.

Even at this hour, the warm November breeze that caressed our faces reminded us of how lucky we were and why we had chosen to come here. After all, we had spent the last week of our time in Canada leaving the taps open just a touch and praying that our pump would not freeze overnight.

It was two long blocks to the main street. There were half a dozen streetlights along the way. One was working - the one on our corner. It was black from there to the avenue but the avenue itself was well lit. The small flashlight attached to my keychain guided us over the speed bumps and past the ruts and holes in the cobblestone street.

This was certainly not Puerto Vallarta. The supermercados - corner stores we would call them back home - the "super" part of their name suggesting more grandeur than they deserved, had closed for the night. The waiters from the restaurants were just completing their cleanup and hauling bags of trash to the curb. The disco at the main intersection of town appeared open; three young men stood outside smoking cigarettes and discussing their options. Apparently, pickings were slim inside. A Volkswagon Beetle drove back and forth blaring dance music from a speaker mounted on its roof; we assumed he was attempting to lure more patrons into the disco but it appeared he was achieving limited success.

There were no gringos on the streets at this hour. It's a retirement community. As we found out much later, one of our favourite watering holes even had its New Years Eve fireworks at eight o'clock because "a lot of people don't make it until midnight."

We walked to the end of the avenue and back. As we stared down the endless dark street to our apartment, we felt strangely calm and safe. Nonetheless, our pace was certainly quick as we made our way home. We had survived the long drive through the blackness from Puerto Vallarta and there would be plenty of time to explore later. Besides, our landlord Kenny had promised us a 'ten peso tour' in the morning.

The Cattle Drive

3.
HOME DELIVERY – MEXICAN STYLE

"Is it open?" Anne asked, as we peered into the darkened structure. "Or do we have the wrong place?"

We had only seen E&R's Bar and Grill from the beach side: a half dozen of the omnipresent white plastic Corona tables under a weathered palapa with a closed in kitchen and a few indoor tables. Our landlord Kenny had recommended it on our 'ten peso tour' of town. But the back entrance was off the main avenue and down a dark and mostly deserted street.

"It has to be open," I replied, "it's Friday night."

The folly of my logic was clear to me the minute the words left my lips. There are two classes of restaurants here: the ones who cater primarily to gringos, which are mostly owned by expats, and the ones whose clientele is largely local. For the former group, I thought, every day must be Friday. It was only much later that I found out that our brains are hardwired from years of waiting for the weekend and, even though all the seasonal residents here are retired or on holidays, business does indeed pick up on Friday and Saturday night.

"Eh, come on in," a voice bellowed from the darkness. "We're open." It was Rosalie, a petite redhead. She turned out to be the 'R' in 'E&R's'. The 'eh' marked her at once as a Canadian.

"The Corona truck was just here," clarified Eddie, the 'E', who we later learned was from Mexico via Oregon, "and he knocked down our power line. Happens once in a while."

The speed with which he applied the electrical tape to the wires and the lack of a shower of sparks told me that it happened more often than Eddie was prepared to admit. A minute later, the lights, such as they were, came on.

As the only patrons for the evening, we chose a table at the window and ordered our meals and two glasses of wine.

"Can you empty your glasses first, please?" Rosalie asked later, when we ordered more wine. "We only have two red wine glasses."

As she headed back to the kitchen for our refill, we made a mental note of what to add to our shopping list for our next excursion to Puerto Vallarta: wine glasses and some decent red wine. For the next six months, finding the latter of the two would prove to be one of our greatest challenges.

"May we join you," asked Eddie after our dinner dishes had been cleared away. He was tall, dark and handsome, just like in the movies.

"It's still early," Rosalie added, as they pulled up two chairs, not bothering to wait for an answer. "A lot of people don't come down until after Christmas."

And over too many Coronas, they told us all about the little community that they called home. What to see. What not to do. Where not to go. Their list had a striking resemblance to the one Kenny had provided on his welcome tour.

"Got wheels?" Eddie asked.

"Come on," said Rosalie, when we answered in the negative, "we'll give you a ride. It's closing time anyway."

Closing time was apparently defined as whenever the last guest headed home or whenever the cold beer ran out, whichever came first. In most cases, I would guess, they happened simultaneously.

"Good choice for dinner," I noted to Anne as we hopped into the back of their Ford pick-up. Eddie and Rosalie sat in the cab with their daughter Christina, who had spent the evening playing on the floor amongst the empty tables.

E&R's Bar and Grill is roughly on the dividing line between the two distinct parts of Guayabitos.

To the north sits the 'Residential Zone'. A wide boulevard cuts through its heart. The boulevard is festooned with hibiscus and bougainvilleas of every colour and description. The road is paved with brick. Roads run off it at all angles, forming a maze of turns and lanes and dead-ends designed, I assume, to discourage fast through traffic. A series of over-sized 'topes' or speed bumps perform this same function on the boulevard.

It is home to million dollar haciendas owned by Canadians and Americans and Mexican lawyers and doctors from Guadalajara. Sprinkled among them are some smaller residences, bought by the old timers before property values began to rise. It is a gated community, lacking only the gates. The winter residents who have neither the inclination nor the money nor both to live there refer to it as 'Gringo Gulch'.

To the south sits 'downtown' Guayabitos.

The entrance to the highway was to the left as we pulled up to the main street: Avenida de Sol Nuevo. We loosened our grip on the sides of the truck, the avenida being the one street in this part of town built with smooth, flat paving stones instead of cobblestones – or worse.

It was the weekend, when the population swells as national tourists arrive from Guadalajara and Tepic, and everyone with a bungalow for rent had parked a pick-up with an ad taped on the back on the entrance road. One truck had their ad neatly printed in the dust on their windshield.

"Resourceful or what," Anne noted.

As we turned right and headed downtown, we surveyed the scene from the bed of the truck. Not that there was anything new. It's barely a fifteen minute walk from one end of the town to the other and we had made the trip before. Several times.

The town plaza sits at the north end of town, just past the entrance off the highway. The town plaza is the hub of any Mexican town. There is invariably a small bandstand in the centre. The bandstand is surrounded by a series of benches, sometimes made of cement and sometimes of wrought iron, all under the shade of the some towering trees. The quality, variety and condition of the shade trees are an indicator of the prosperity of the community. The benches are usually filled with local seniors during the day, seeking shade from the hot sun, and young lovers at night, seeking shade from their parents.

But there are few Mexicans who actually live full time in Guayabitos. They live in the neighbouring towns of La Peñita or La Colonia or the little villages up in the mountains beyond. So, on most days and nights, the plaza sits largely empty, save for the occasional Huitol Indian who has come to town to sell their handicrafts by day and sleep in the band shell by night.

There are exceptions, we found out later that year. There is a car show in the fall and every February the Guayabitos Hotel Owners Association who, for all intents and purposes runs the town, puts on free shows for the tourists, and the square is packed. They'd feature a classical string quartet or a percussion band that used nothing but tin cans as instruments. Most shows would end with a folk dance performance replete with beautiful young señoritas in colourful, twirling skirts and macho young men juggling razor-sharp machetes over their heads and between their legs while blindfolded. One night they had a Men's Choir and I could only assume that the sopranos were the guys who didn't make the cut, so to speak, as machete twirlers.

We had rented a post box at the Post Office that sits behind the plaza for $14 a year. I guess we were in the minority; Sergio the Postmaster would always take time to give us a little wave as he rode by on his little red scooter. The Mexican Postal Service is re-nowned for its efficiency – or lack thereof. It takes anywhere from two weeks to several months for a letter to arrive from Canada, so we're not sure what method of transport they use.

The post office is open from 8:00 to 4:00. It's only slightly larger than a phone booth, with several rows of neatly polished stainless steel mailboxes, most of them empty, along one wall. Sometimes 4:00 becomes 3:00 or 2:30 but Sergio always leaves a note. Our favourite was "Post Office Closed – I've Gone to Get the Mail".

As in every Mexican city and town, a Catholic Church sits adjacent to the plaza. It is a deeply religious country and people make the sign of the cross as they walk or drive past the church. The Guayabitos church looks strangely out of place. It is modern with smooth lines, little in way of adornments and an art-deco spire.

It is so unlike the colonial churches we have seen in other small towns. There is not much history here.

A 'Cake Lady' stood behind a folding card table still half full of scrumptious flan and two layer slices of rich chocolate three milk cake, as we lumbered down the avenue in the bed of Eddie and Rosalie's pick-up that night. Every Friday and Saturday, local ladies would come to town and set card tables on the side of the street, where they sell huge slices of heaven for $1.50. The aroma of vanilla and cocoa and caramel filled the air. If we had been walking, we would have stopped for sure, but we hated to impose on the hospitality of Rosalie and Eddie.

A police Pick-up truck passed us on the other side of the boulevard. Two officers sat in the open back, AK47's at the ready. They have all kinds of police here: Federal Police, State Police, Municipal Police and 'Tourist Police'. While it's pretty clear what the first three do, I am not sure what the role of the Tourist Police is; it must be to arrest gringos who don't buy enough cheap, junky Mexican souvenirs. A line I had read in our Mexican tour book came to mind:

> "Like any large Mexican city, Guadalajara has countless police troops with overlapping municipal, state and federal jurisdictions. In an emergency, don't call any one of them – it would only increase the possibility that no one will show up."

So in spite of, rather than because of, the presence of so many law enforcement officials, we had come to feel very safe here; our early fears were behind us. We walked everywhere at night, although we did carry a flashlight. While there is certainly property crime, as one would expect in a community with so huge a gap between rich and poor, we have heard of virtually no violent crime. I have no doubt that it must exist, but we had encountered no-one who had been its victim.

But we did know people who had had encounters with the police. It was shortly after we had arrived when word made its way through the North Americano community. In a somewhat ironic twist, Mexican Immigration officials had raided twenty-five businesses here. It seems that Canadians and Americans had been sneaking across the border on Tourist Visas to work illegally at $5 a day waitressing jobs. They were young women who spent their summers working at places like Wasaga Beach in Ontario or the Poconos to raise enough money to spend a winter down here, hoping to soak up as much sun, and drink as much beer, as they could between shifts. I guess you have to wonder just who that giant wall that President Bush was building alongside the Rio Grande was intended to protect.

Crico's Supermercado sits further along at the main intersection of town, where Avenida del Sol Nuevo meets the second exit to the highway, and the town's second traffic light. It has the best selection of imported foodstuffs: things like instant potatoes and seafood sauce and, despite the fact we have yet to see an Asian face, one of the largest collections of oriental sauces and seasonings that I have seen anywhere. They also have lots of uniquely Mexican items: vanilla-cinnamon and piña colada Crystal Lite.; gummi chicken feet and potato chip flavours like cheese and lime and chili. You can get pretty well anything here with lime and chili – coconut, pineapple, shrimp snacks. I suspect, if you made a special request, the cake ladies would even serve it on your flan.

There are no gringocentric restaurants on the Avenida; instead, they are relegated to the highway or La Peñita or the dark back streets. It's the first come first serve principle at work. But there are lots of restaurants with a more national client base. They grill steak and chicken and onions and peppers on open gas-fired grills along the sidewalk. They line up plastic chairs on the side of the road for their customers. They serve tacos and enchiladas and quesadillas on melmac plates that they wrap in plastic so they can be used for the next customer with no need for cleaning.

The aromas are intoxicating but we have learned to resist temptation. One night Anne tried a roasted jalapeno pepper from a street vendor.

"No es picante," the server assured us solemnly. But the sly smile told us otherwise.

Anne quickly spit it out, but she still couldn't feel her tongue for three days.

As we came to our street, we moved to signal Eddie but we saw instantly that there was no need. He knew exactly where we lived and had already started the turn onto Avenida Gardenias.

There was little to see on the main street beyond Avenida Gardenias. The landscape was dominated by Decamaron Los Cocos, the largest all-inclusive resort in the area: a maze of brightly coloured buildings that caters mostly to Canadians and Americans.

Without direction, Eddie pulled up in front of the apartment.

"If there is anything we can do for you," he offered as we climbed out of the back of the truck, "don't hesitate to ask."

After thanks and goodbyes, we watched the tail lights bounce up and down as the truck made its way out to the highway to Los Ayala. And then they disappeared and we stood in silence in the dim light of the one working street lamp.

We smiled at each other as we unlocked the wrought iron gate.

I think we're going to like this place.

4.
THE DENTAL PLAN

I had a hankering for a bagel: a fresh toasted bagel with melted cheese, served on our balcony with a steaming cup of the aromatic local coffee. My mouth was already watering as Anne and I stood waiting on the sidewalk. It was January 6, a date I would have to remember for next year.

We had been making a pilgrimage to Puerto Vallarta about every second week, sometimes even more often than that. There were certain food items that we couldn't find anywhere in Jaltemba Bay: orange cheddar cheese, decent red wines, T-bone steaks, light margarine — for that strict low-cholesterol diet of ours — and bagels. But it had been a while since our last trip, as we had waited for the Christmas rush to subside. Our supplies were running low.

We had heard all kinds of horror stories about how busy Guayabitos would be Christmas Week. But it was our landlord Kenny's tale of how one year Laura had rented out a storage closet to a couple from Guadalajara, who could find no other accommodation, which had caused us the most discomfort.

But there had been an eerie silence on Christmas Day. It seemed a day like any other. The stores were almost all open and we even had garbage pick-up. Mind you, one of the garbage men was dressed in a gorilla suit but, oddly enough, that seemed a lot less strange to us than it would have a month or so earlier. Christmas here is, above all, a religious holiday not a time for Santa Claus and lavish gifts.

We had heard some commotion Christmas night but it in no way prepared us for what we saw the next morning.

We had been the only tenants in our four unit building up to that point. "A lot of people don't come down until after Christmas," Rosalie had told us. But by morning, an entire tour bus full of families from Guadalajara was crammed into the three other units. Beach towels hung everywhere. We maneuvered through the beach chairs and water toys in the courtyard to head downtown.

Our little three block street might see a dozen cars a busy afternoon but on that day we counted twenty-five buses. They were nose to tail all the way down the street. Black fumes choked the air as we made out way down the gauntlet to the main avenida. Drivers slept soundly in the luggage compartments, unable or unwilling to pay for a room.

Christmas in Mexico had required some compromise on our part. Our traditional tourtiere on Christmas Eve gave way to the last of our Puerto Vallarta T-bone steaks. I had to make my corned beef hash Christmas breakfast with hot Mexican Chorizo instead.

We couldn't find Christmas stockings so we filled Christmas hats in their place, which proved to be a blessing, as it was hard enough finding sufficient junk to even fill a hat.

Most of our gifts proved to be underwhelming at best. Anne stumbled upon her big gift, hidden under the bed, on Christmas Eve while chasing a gecko out of the spare bedroom. The cloth Frisbee with the hole in the middle proved to be a less than stellar feat of engineering and our Mexican playing cards turned out to only have numbers one through twelve, no face cards, and four suits: swords, medals, crowns and footstools.

The one successful gift was our Lotteria game. Lotteria is Mexican bingo, except that, instead of numbers, the cards have pictures of different objects, with their Spanish definition superimposed.

"It will be a good way to learn Spanish," Anne suggested.

And while we learned words like el camaron (shrimp) and el pescado (fish), which did prove useful in conversation, it will probably be difficult to work el negrito (the negro) or el burrocho (the drunk) into a sentence. Besides, the el negrito square had a particularly troubling but uncanny resemblance to Al Jolson.

We also managed to have a traditional Christmas dinner, turkey with all the trimmings, at a local restaurant on the beach. A band regaled us with traditional Spanish ballads like 'All Shook Up', 'Wasted Days and Wasted Nights' and 'Silhouettes in the Shade'.

But Christmas was behind us now. The families from inland had headed home and new neighbours from north of the border now occupied the other three units of our building.

And we were off to Puerto Vallarta in search of supplies. Getting to PV, as the locals call it, is an all day adventure.

"I think that's one," Anne said hopefully as we caught sight of the white van making its way down the street.

'One' would mean a collectivo: a unique Mexican form of transportation. It's a Volkswagon van that seats eight comfortably but rarely carries less than a dozen people. Passengers sit four to a seat, or in the doorway, or on each other's lap, or on a wooden crate set in between the driver's and the passenger's seat. For fifty cents, you can travel from one end of Jaltemba Bay to the other.

Not all white vans here are collectivos of course, but people tend to hail down any white van that passes in the hope that it is. Sometimes the vans marked 'collectivo' are really taxis; sometimes vans marked 'taxi' are really collectivos. It's all a rather hit and miss proposition.

Luck was with us and we crammed our way into the van as it pulled over to the side of the road.

The collectivo took us to the Pacifico Bus Terminal in La Peñita where we caught the second class bus to PV. There is no first class bus that you can take from here; first class buses come complete with comfortable seats, a TV that shows recent movies and a stewardess who serves 'in-flight' meals. The second class bus has lesser creature comforts. The seats are spartan but generally functional and, unlike the third class buses, there is no livestock in the passenger compartment. Sometimes, there is even a TV showing old black and white movies. With no stewardess to help out, we watched in horror on one trip as the driver got up and stood in the aisle adjusting the volume as the bus kept on rolling down the highway.

Bus service is certainly frequent enough since La Peñita sits on the routes from PV to both Tepic and Guadalajara but the schedule is a work of pure fiction. The buses get there when they get there. The next inter-city bus is always "in twenty minutes", but sometimes twenty minutes means five and sometimes it means sixty.

A quick hop off the Pacifico bus before it headed off the highway to the main terminal led us to the last step of the journey: the 'Centro' city bus to downtown. Unlike their inter-city cousins, city buses tend to save maintenance costs by shedding extras like shocks and springs. Buskers play guitars or accordions or harmonicas. Others hawk restaurants or charities.

"I'm sure they get paid by commission," I told Anne, as the bus lurched from stop to stop, the driver racing to beat his colleagues to the next batch of potential riders.

Canadians and Americans are used to having a Walmart in every city and town of consequence. In fact, it is not unusual, for the local populace to fight to keep them out for fear that they will drive the local merchants out of business. But in Mexico, the appearance of a Walmart was a godsend to the Nord Americanos who spent a large chunk of the winter here.

There had been no Walmart the last time we had traveled to Puerto Vallarta several years before. There was a Ley's Supermarket at the edge of downtown which was well past its prime; it was old and grungy, with empty boxes littering the aisle and as much produce on the floor as there was on the shelves. And there was an El Gigante which was neat and clean but, at least at that time, was stocked almost entirely with non-imported products. And then there were a number of smaller supermercados similar to what we had in Guayabitos, except that they were even more primitive at that time.

When you are visiting somewhere for a brief holiday, it is fun to shun the same foods you buy back home and to exist only on meat and produce and dry goods that are native to the country that is serving as your host. But the novelty had worn off by about week four.

The Puerto Vallarta Walmart was clean and bright and new. It was a precursor of the Superstores that we now have back home. Anne and I checked our backpacks at the Paqueteria, knowing that they would soon be filled with all kinds of wondrous new things that we would slog back on the bus to Guayabitos.

The produce section featured all the fruits and vegetables that we had become accustomed to seeing: avocado and tomatillo, chayote and jicama, a dozen kinds of peppers, and bananas, melons, oranges and manguey. But there were also pink lady apples and bartlett pears and freestone peaches, all with that 'Product of US' sticker.

There was a fish market and a meat section which featured what was at least advertised to be Alberta beef, at a fraction of what we pay in Canada. We loaded up on as many of the huge T-bones at four bucks a piece as we thought we could cram into our backpacks.

Back in Guayabitos, the only cold cut we could find was ham, although they do stock a number of varieties. There must have been fifty different kinds of ham here. And besides that, there was. Well, actually there was little else but that huge array of ham.

"These are all the same wines that we can buy back in town," Anne moaned as we wandered through the rows of the liquor aisle.

"Preference?" I asked.

"I'm not that much of a wine snob. I'll take anything that says 'Product of France' or 'Product of Australia' or 'Product of Anywhere Where They Don't Speak Spanish'."

We settled on one Australian red we found with a penguin on the label; the name was unfamiliar but it would have to do. We grabbed two bottles.

But at least we could peruse the liquor section.

"Razor theft is clearly on the rise here," I noted as I sorted through the empty boxes stacked in the pharmacy.

34

"You take the empty box to the service counter by the entrance," the clerk patiently explained. "They will give you the actual blades."

Our cart was full as we headed for our last stop: the bakery.

"I have no idea how we are going to load all of this into our two backpacks," I sighed as I stared at the full cart.

"We can probably carry two extra bags each."

I grimaced at the thought of juggling packages and backpacks on the hour and a half bus ride home.

"I'll pass on the pastry and the fresh French loaf but I'll be damned if I'm going to home without any bagels."

They had been in my dreams since early that morning.

There is a large bakery at the Walmart in Puerto Vallarta; there are half a dozen aisles of breads and rolls and pastries and cookies. I rushed to the counter to pick up the silver tray and tongs that you use to make your selections.

The first row was floor to ceiling with boxes of something labeled 'Rosca de Reyes'. I picked one up. It looked like one of the Christmas tea rings that we used to buy every year back home.

"Looks good," I noted, "but it's too big to carry home."

The second aisle was more of the same. And the third. And the fourth. The fifth. The sixth. There was only one item that day in six aisles of baked goods at the Puerto Vallarta Walmart: 'Rosca de Reyes.'

"It means 'Ring of the King,'" Kenny explained as we sat on the balcony later that night while I commiserated over a rum and coke. "It's a tradition on the Feast of the Epiphany."

"And that's today: January 6?" I asked, proudly recalling an early Sunday school lesson.

"Exactly," Kenny replied."

"They bake a plastic Baby Jesus into it, everyone has a slice, and whoever bites into the Baby Jesus must make tamales for all their friends," Laura added.

In Canada when they find bits of plastic in Cadbury Easter Eggs they do a major recall; here they plant them on purpose to assign kitchen duty.

As I sat there staring into the dark night, I was thinking about a conversation I had had the day before with an American friend of mine. He had just signed up for the IMSS, the Mexico health plan.

"For $170 a year, anyone who can show proof of residency, which can be as little as a power bill, gets full medical coverage," he had told me. "And that includes dental coverage."

Maybe dental coverage isn't a bad thing to have when they are burying hunks of plastic in their pastry.

5.
CROCODILE TEARS

The Door to Nowhere

"Can you tell what it is?" I asked.

"It looks like a palapa," Anne replied, "but I can't be sure."

We shaded our eyes against the blazing afternoon sun. We could make out something perhaps five kilometers off in the distance but we had no idea what it was. As I looked back, the last vestiges of La Peñita were beginning to fade from view.

"We must be half way there," I offered, "we might as well see what it is."

I wiped the sweat from my brow and gulped another swig of water before passing the bottle to Anne. The deep blue Pacific Ocean, mere steps away, looked cool and inviting but the waves were high and the drop-off was steep. There was no-one swimming on this part of the beach. In fact, there was no-one here at all.

The last people we had seen were back at the 'Fred Flintstone' house, just before the turtle farm. The house had an outdoor kitchen and living room and pool. Its lines were rough and the cement walls were a soft yellow. A small patch of lawn separated the outside living area from what we assumed were a couple of bedrooms. I'm not quite sure why we called it that. It just somehow looked prehistoric. And when we mentioned the 'Fred Flintstone' house to our neighbours Pat and Bruce, they knew instantly which house we meant.

But even that was a couple of kilometers back now, just a small patch of yellow buried back in the palm trees that framed the beach.

Guayabitos Beach is a gorgeous expanse of white sand, with a slow gentle slope out into the ocean. It bills itself as the largest wading pool in the world. The south end of the beach is quiet during the week but gets busy on the weekend. The north end, the part that runs alongside the millionaire homes of Gringo Gulch, sits virtually empty most of the year, except of course for Christmas and Semana Santa.

We had spent a lot of time on Guayabitos Beach that year: lying in the sun, reading, people watching. We had watched the vendors struggle through the soft sand with carts so laden down with air mattresses and beach balls and inflatable whales that we had no idea how they managed to wind their way down the beach without running over or through everyone in their path. We had inhaled the tempting fragrance of shrimp and fish grilling over wood fires on portable grills. We had marveled at the plates of coconut macaroons that sellers placed so close to your face that you could almost taste them. We listened to the all-to-familiar song from the ice cream cart as it bicycled past.

And we turned away as an old lady approached with beads and string and a binder of photos of her braiding designs. Anne had learned the hard way that there are some things you should not scrimp on when she spent a week looking like Buckwheat after getting her hair braided by a vendor named Larry. It took an hour to get it done and two days to get it unbraided the next week.

But today, we had both been bored of just lying on the beach and had decided to go for a walk. We had walked the length of Guayabitos Beach, past the fading, white wooden door that had aroused our curiosity on many occasions: the one that stood at the top of a short flight of stairs and led literally to nowhere. We had waded through the ankle-deep estuary that separates Guayabitos from La Peñita.

We had made our way down the length of the beach in La Peñita, a true working beach. Pelicans darted and dove for the remnants the fishermen leave on the beach and the air was punctuated by the roar of the fishermen gunning their engines as they ram their boats as far onto the shore as they could, before tying them up to a house or a tree or, occasionally, a post on the far side of the road.

We had made the short but tricky climb up the slippery volcano rock outcropping to the north that brings you to La Colonia beach. And now we stood halfway down that long sliver of sand and tried to figure out whether or not to keep going.

One of our favourite treats on the beach was a pineapple bowl. They slice the top off a pineapple and fill it all variety of wondrous and conflicting flavours: crushed pineapple, watermelon, cucumber, jicama, grenadine, lime juice, salt, chili. The grenadine invariably leaks through and stains your hands; it is truly a three napkin snack. I lusted for one now as the soft sand cliffs collapsed beneath our feet.

The silence and solitude was both relaxing and disquieting.

"Do you think we should be here?" Anne asked.

"I didn't see any warning signs," I replied, knowing full well that we wouldn't have been able to understand them even if there were.

"There is a naval base in Guayabitos," I added only half in jest, "maybe this is what they use for artillery target practice."

It was three hours later, just past one o'clock when we reached the end of the beach. It wasn't a palapa after all that we had seen from down the beach; it was a whole community of them. Half a dozen beach restaurants set in the middle of nowhere - a ten kilometer walk down a lonely, desolate stretch of beach.

Fish never tasted so good. It was red snapper, grilled whole, in garlic. Even the beady eyes staring back at me, pleading, were not enough to discourage me from digging in. The beer was cold and wet.

"Another?" the young waiter asked as we gulped down our second round of Coronas. It was a long walk home and our desire to avoid dehydration trumped our inclination to more thoroughly relieve our parched throats.

"No, gracias" I replied before adding "dos aquas por favor," as I pointed to the two empty bottles of water that we had drained on the way in.

He was certainly on the underside of twelve and I was struck by the fluency of his English. The vocabulary of most of the kids his age in town was limited to 'hello' and 'how are you?' And here he was living at the end of a deserted beach being able to form rudimentary sentences.

"Finish?" he asked as he stared at plates piled high with bones and skin – and heads.

"Like see my crocodile?' he asked eagerly.

Anne and I stared at each other. We tried to politely decline but his big brown eyes told us that 'no' was not an acceptable answer.

Gathering up the bones, he motioned us to follow him through the kitchen and out to the lagoon that ran behind the row of restaurants. The splash of the bones as they hit the water was alarm enough. The tall grass along the side of the lagoon came to life as three enormous crocodiles slithered out in search of lunch.

They all had names that our young friend pronounced slowly, for our benefit, as he pointed them out one by one. The Spanish names meant nothing to us; for all we knew they might have been the Spanish equivalents of 'Spot' and 'Fido' and 'Prince."

As we girded ourselves for the long walk home, a voice from the restaurant next door caught our attention.

"When do we see the crocs?" the voice asked in perfect English,

I spun around in surprise. There sat a man I recognized at Raoul at a table with half a dozen gringos, none of whom were familiar to me. We had seen Rauol often at the beach in Guayabitos, hawking tours to the hot springs and to San Blas, and to the crocodile farm. And as I turned fully around, I caught sight of his van: the beat-up old yellow and white Volkswagon van, with 'Tours' roughly painted in large black letters. It sat at the end of a dusty road, which I now knew led out to the highway, the one that headed south to Guayabitos.

6.
OU MEXICAN JOUNAL

"Damn donkey," I cursed as I hooked my drive into the rough. "He bayed half way through my backswing."

"Now that's an excuse you don't hear every day," laughed Anne. "Don't worry. I spotted your ball. It's halfway between the coconut husk and that cactus."

There was a nine hole pitch and putt golf course about five minutes down the road by taxi. For twenty bucks you can play all day although, with the heat, I doubt if many people last more than eighteen holes. There were some unique Mexican hazards. I got one ball stuck in the middle of a cactus plant. The leaves were as sharp as razor blades; perhaps even sharper than the cheap Brazilian-made disposable blades that they sell here.

"So what do you do all day?" It's a question that anyone who has ever retired has had to answer.

I know; I've asked it many times to the old timers who came back to the office to visit. The ones you were pleasant enough to, but who you secretly hoped would go away so that you could get back to work.

"Don't really know, but I sure am busy," is the answer they invariably gave.

And then they would always add with a smirk, just to torture you for asking the question in the first place: "I'm not sure how I ever fit work into my schedule."

For us, in our first year in Guayabitos, golf was a small part of the answer. Going to the beach was a big component, as was biking and hiking.

And then there were the fundraisers. Like the horseshoe tournament they have every year on the beach, where the toughest part was finding the shoes when they got buried in the beach sand. Or the annual tour of the Thomas Bartlett Estate. Or the dessert buffet to aid the school in Las Ayala, where my precautions for the dark walk home gave Anne the opportunity to ask: "Is that a flashlight in your pocket or are you just glad to see me?"

But by far the biggest part of our days here was spent just doing 'stuff.' 'Stuff' just takes longer to do down here.

In Canada, shopping for groceries is a minor irritation – something you spend half an hour doing on the way home from work. In Mexico, grocery shopping is just one big scavenger hunt that sometimes takes days and can even involve traveling from town to town.

It's amazing how excited people get when they do find rare items. One day I was almost bowled over when someone realized that I had found an English language newspaper in La Peñita, even if it was a three day old Miami Herald. And you could actually hear the buzz of excitement when pretzels first showed up on the shelves of Crico's Supermercado.

"Carol and Frank are coming over for dinner," Anne had informed me one morning. "What do you want to make?"

"Jambalaya," I responded after some thought. It was a specialty of mine and the main ingredients, shrimp and chicken and sausage, could all be procured without the necessity of a trip to PV.

The 'hunt' began with a 6:00 AM wake-up call and a trip to the beach. There were three boats hauled up on the shore that day; each packed with ice and weight scales, shrimp and red snapper and mahi mahi. The fish they had caught themselves; the shrimp they had merely hauled from the shrimp boats that were always anchored out by the big island that marked the centre of Jaltemba Bay.

I had learned from experience that there was an art to this. I looked thoughtfully through the selection of fresh fish and seafood in the first boat; marking time, pretending to decide what our morning's purchase would be. When the young señorita in the long-sleeved yellow dress began to point at the tub of jumbo shrimp, I saw my opportunity and stepped smartly in behind her.

"Cuánto cuesto?" she asked. *"How much?"*

I wasn't entirely sure what the answer was but I thought I heard "ocho" – *eight* – in there somewhere.

She waited patiently as the vendor scooped a few handfuls of the large succulent shrimp onto the old rusted metal scale. Her eyes never left the scale.

"Lo mismo," I said proudly as my turn came up. *The same.* I held up two fingers and watched as he weighed out my two kilograms of shrimp and grudgingly took my money. Our purchase cost about $17 Canadian.

"I'm never paying the gringo price again," I chuckled to Anne as we made our way to the next stop.

Roberto the butcher was a rotund man with a quick smile. He had studied as an architect but married into the meat business. We had become friends the day he saw us lugging two jugs of water home and gave us a ride in his truck.

"Coronas?" I said, more as a question than a request, as I held up four fingers. He smiled as he placed four Corona Sausages into a plastic bag.

"Sausage?" he asked proudly, always eager to practice his English as he handed me a small square of poster board and a felt marker. He smiled broadly and shook my hand as I carefully spelled it out for him to hang up in the shop.

I checked off another item on the list. The butcher shops here sold only beef and pork, not chicken; chicken would require a quick bike trip to La Peñita where two ladies have tables set out on the main avenida. The chickens; legs, feet, gizzards and all, are kept in a glass case in the hot sun, so we try to buy early in the morning.

Don Pedros had the rice but no peppers; the vegetable market two doors down had red but not green peppers; Super Lorena, much to our delight, had both green peppers and cayenne pepper in a small cellophane pack. But when the cayenne pepper turned out to be paprika instead, it was back to Cricos.

It was the last item that proved to be most complicated: a new plastic cutting board. A vigorous game of charades produced first a knife, then a mixing bowl, then a package of bandages before that eureka moment when a cutting board arrived on the counter.

Luckily, we still had one bottle left of that Australian red wine with the penguin on the label that we had saved from our last excursion to PV.

It was almost two when we finally made it back to the apartment with the last of our goodies. Just in time for a bite and a quick siesta to recover from our early morning wake-up call, before it would be time to start making dinner.

But it's not just shopping that took longer. Getting your email messages meant not just sitting down at your desk for a minute but a three block walk to the internet café and a ten minute wait for one of the working machines to be free. Making a phone call back to Canada didn't mean just picking up the receiver and dialing. It meant buying a phone card, or two, and searching for a public phone that was both working and outside shouting range of the gas truck and the other assorted vendors that cruise the streets.

And as for dealing with the government, you were best advised to pack a suitcase.

Upon arrival in Mexico, all visitors are issued a Tourist Card: an official looking document that is signed and stamped and needs to be surrendered before you leave the country. And since ours said 90 days and our stay was to be much longer, it was some time in January when we decided to make the long trek to PV to get them extended.

Or should that be treks. While we found the Immigration Office on our first attempt, it turned out that they closed at 1:00 PM and we had missed them by half an hour. With an hour time difference between PV and Guayabitos, and an hour's ride to get there, we took no chances the next day; we caught the 6:00 AM bus.

The office was full when we got there, as was the hallway. When we pulled ticket number 64 from the little dispenser and we heard the officer call 32, we knew that the odds of a third trek loomed large. It was almost noon when they called our number. But we were ready.

"You have to make copies of the forms," the nice older lady from Oregon had told us as we sat together waiting. "And your passports. Every page. Even the blank ones."

"You can get copies at the pharmacy downstairs," someone else had chimed in.

And as I had waited for Anne to get the copies, I couldn't help but wonder what relationship the owner of the pharmacy was to the Minister of Immigration. Photocopying was clearly a pretty good business.

I rushed to the counter as they called out our number and proudly plunked down the copies and our $40 fee.

The official studied them carefully, making sure that every empty page of our passports was copied.

"We don't take cash here," he somberly intoned. "You have to go to the bank."

I looked at my watch and mumbled something about La Peñita and two days and a Pacifico bus.

"I will wait here," he smiled.

It was almost 1:00 when we returned after a bus ride to the bank and a taxi back and some wild gesturing through the locked glass office door to get his attention.

Yes, 'stuff' just takes longer here.

As we rode home on the bus, with our new Tourist Cards clutched firmly in hand, we reminisced about another encounter with Mexican bureaucracy. This time it was in the private sector.

Our friend Bob was visiting us at our timeshare at the Sheraton. We were checking out Saturday morning but Bob had a midnight flight on Friday. They have a simple but effective check-out system. When you pay your bill, they give you a little chit and they won't let you leave the lobby with your luggage until you surrender it. That ensures that no-one leaves without paying.

"Ticket?" the bellhop had asked as Bob wheeled his luggage through the empty lobby and began to hail a cab.

"Mañana. Our apartment." We tried all manner of explanations but the young man would have none of it.

And finally, as frustrations rose and departure time drew nigh, the bellhop pulled a sheet of paper from the desk, wrote 'paid' and handed it to himself. And then he smiled broadly as he flagged down a taxi for our guest.

"I should put that together with our trip to Immigration," I said, "and put it in the next journal,"

I had been keeping a journal of all the wild and wacky things that we had come across during our stay down here. Of course sending it home meant a trip to the internet café. So every couple of weeks, we would trudge down there, diary in hand, and pick out the best bits to send to our friends back home. We called it 'Our Mexican Journal'.

We eventually even figured out how to add pictures to the text. Since the keyboards and all the software were in Spanish, it took a bit of doing and I mostly had to go by memory. And some of the keyboards were a little worn; the "r" didn't work on computer number nine. I had to be extra careful when I was assigned to that machine to make sure that the next volume wouldn't be entitled 'Ou Mexican Jounal'.

I had just finished typing up the last installment, the one about our visit to Immigration and our hike down a deserted beach to the crocodile farm. And as our pictures made their way back through cyberspace to Canada, I decided to check out Jaltemba Bay Folk. It's a message board run with postings on everything from 'Looking for a Ride to PV' to 'What Time Does the Entertainment Start'. The latest posting caught my attention:

> *Crocodile Warning*
> *Keep an eye on your dogs when you're walking them on the beach in La Colonia. The crocodiles are very active.*

No wonder the beach was so deserted. Security must be a little lax at the crocodile farm.

And as I walked home from the internet café that night, that old World War I song kept running through my head: "How you gonna keep them down on the farm after they've ate Fluf-fy."

7.
THE BEST LAID PLANS

We had figured it all out about ten years before. On the way back from our day trip to 'Why A Bee Toes'. We would spend our first year of retirement there. Then maybe the next year it would be Thailand or Australia or maybe even just Florida.

So if we only had one year here, we wanted to see it all. We set ourselves a goal of seeing one town a week: by bus or collective, or by bike or on foot. We expected more of the same, but they each had their little quirks and foibles.

We started with the beach towns.

Sayulita is a surfer town. Quaint little boutiques line the main street and it seems like every third store is a surf shop. The signs are all in English and the town is packed with young virile gringos with that tanning bed look who come up by bus from PV for the day. The beach vendors sell hash pipes along with the usual fare of jewelry and beach umbrellas and little onyx figurines.

"I'm sure that it's no coincidence that Rollie's Restaurant's here", Anne noted as we pondered our choices at the place which serves the best breakfasts in this part of the country.

It's a lively place that's always packed and has a menu with the look and feel of Grateful Dead album cover.

San Francisco/San Pancho is the yuppy capital of Riviera Nayarit. The streets are paved with, well not exactly gold but at least brick, as compared to the cobblestones, or worse, that adorn the roads in most of the area's towns. The Mexicans call the place San Pancho; the Americans, San Francisco. But then every person here named Francisco is nicknamed Pancho and every Jesus is Chuy. I guess it makes as much sense to us, as all Roberts being Bobs or Henrys being Hanks does to our Mexican friends. As is often the case here, the Americans have won, at least officially, according to the maps and the road signs. There are gated communities and an exclusive resort that keeps the riff raff off the beach.

While San Francisco has two names, Lo de Marcos is, in some ways, two towns. There is a small, older town with a few shops where the locals live. And then there is a string of RV parks that stretch the length of the beach. It's a quiet little community since; as they do elsewhere, RVers tend to make their own entertainment.

And then there is Chacala, the place where old hippies go to retire; the sixties were very good to the town's residents. It's a gorgeous beach set beside a small, quiet town but the cornerstone of the community is the holistic healing centre that sits at the south end of the beach. Anne and I had tried to recreate the sculptures that centre residents had made along the shore: jagged rocks, piled four high, each one somehow delicately balanced on top of the one below. I guess you needed some of those holistic healing skills to learn how to do it. Either that or a weekly trip to Sayulita to replenish your supplies from the beach vendors selling the funny looking pipes.

After we had seen all the beach towns, it was time to venture inland.

Our first such trip was to El Tonino. It sits about 6 kms off the highway up in the mountains. It was a pleasant enough bike ride along the highway, past the ostrich farm and the Guayabitos airport. The airport consists of a single lane of asphalt, a windsock and a plain white concrete farmhouse set on ten foot high concrete piers. The farmhouse is distinguished by an over-sized casita on the roof and a gigantic picture window. The whole concoction surrounded by a high and surprisingly well-maintained chain link fence.

However, 'pleasant' would be that last word that would come to mind as we crossed the highway and started up the road to El Tonino. The 'road', and I use the term loosely, like the gravel that adorned it, ran up the mountain - straight up the mountain. We had biked maybe one kilometer, and pushed the bikes another two, when we stumbled upon a small orchard of papaya trees and decided that it would be a lot faster to chain up the bikes and continue on foot.

It was a quaint little town of perhaps five hundred souls with ramshackle houses and million dollar views. The two village cows mooed gently off in the distance as we entered the village. Kids smiled broadly and whispered among themselves, as kids do, about the two strange gringos and what reasons they might have for venturing into El Tonino.

The trip home provided its own set of challenges. The bikes lurched from bump to bump as our stark white knuckles pushed down hard on the brakes. A truckload full of kids cheered us on as the driver swerved to pass us. We watched intently for the three donkeys tied up to an old weathered banyon tree that was our sign that we were about to roar across busy Highway 200, if the fellow at the bike shop hadn't adjusted the brakes as he had promised.

We didn't bother with our bikes for our next inland trip, the one to Alta Vista. Collectivos run regularly between La Peñita and Las Varas, the next major town. The sign said 'Alta Vista - 6 kms' as we called for the driver to let us off on the side of the highway, but then I think that the signs all say '6 kms'. It's really just a best guess. Just like the best guess we had to make ourselves a little later when we came to a fork on the road; we could vaguely make out something high up in the mountains that could be a town and since 'Alta' means 'high', we went right.

"Buenos dias," the farmer called out as eased the black pick-up truck to a stop beside us. The vehicle had clearly spent many hours on this rutted and dusty road.

He motioned with his thumb to the bed of the truck and we eagerly clambered in.

"People pay big bucks for a view like this," Anne said, as we later sat sipping cokes on the town square and gazing down at the tiny speck that was La Peñita, lost next to the vast expanse of the Pacific.

Hiking trails wound themselves around the top of the mountain. A sickly sweet smell assaulted our nostrils as we wandered past a tiny hovel hidden back in the trees. And we wondered if the 'Alta' in the town's name referred to something other than the altitude.

We had just started the long descent home, having noted that our new friend in the black pick-up was enjoying a couple of Pacifico Beers on the steps of the local supermercado and clearly in no rush to leave And while we had come to expect the unexpected in Mexico, this one was beyond the pale.

"Guayabitos?" the taxi driver asked as he pulled up beside us.

It was a good guess and we dared ask no questions as we nodded 'yes'. There stood a taxi, marked La Peñita, out here in the middle of nowhere, going just where we wanted to go. But then maybe it was no coincidence at all. Word travels fast in a small town. Where else could two poor lost white folks be going?

With the small towns all checked off our list, it was time to venture into the cities. Tepic is the capital of the state of Nayarit. It's a modern and clean city, with its economy based on government and education rather than tourism, so we had decided that it was worth an overnight trip.

It was a beautiful, albeit nerve-wracking, bus ride from La Peñita to Tepic. The road twists and turns up and down two mountains. Anne and I gawked in awe at the dramatic scenery: high peaks and plummeting valleys. But it's funny what you get used and how mundane the things you see every day become. The Mexicans on the bus simply closed the drapes to keep out the sun and dozed fitfully.

While it's not an express bus, there are only three stops along the way. There is Las Varas, which we remembered for its many butcher shops. It was something we had attributed to the fact that it's the first town of any consequence north of Puerto Vallarta that wasn't on the ocean; by the time people reach it, they must have had their fill of sea food. There is Compostela, a cowboy city, where every third or fourth store seems to be is a saddle shop. And then there is the fruit and vegetable checkpoint, where, for reasons unbeknownst to us, soldiers armed with AK47s inspect every vehicle to ensure that no-one is bringing fresh produce into the interior of the country.

The reason that there are only three stops is not the fact that the Pacifico Bus Company wants to ensure that their customers get there as quickly as possible. It's the fact that there is absolutely nowhere else to stop.

We stayed at a lovely hotel: Fray Junipero Serra. It was quaint yet modern, with almost a European feel to it. It sat in the heart of downtown, across from a lovely and lively plaza. And the beautiful and historic Cathedral of the Purísima Concepción de María was just across the street. The charming bells from the cathedral echoed from the plaza as it counted out each quarter hour.

By 11:30 PM the tolling of the bells had become somewhat less charming and by 2:15 in the morning, they were downright annoying. With sleep a distant memory, I searched the room for anything to read, the more boring the better. A pamphlet from the hotel caught my eye. The English translation was rough and stilted which I considered a good thing at this point since it would be more likely to cause my eyes to glaze over.

> "Tepic was founded in the 1750's by an excommunicated monk - Fray Junipero Serra – for whom this hotel was named. Fray Junipero Serra literally translates as 'Crazy Brother from the Mountains'."

Maybe it was the church bells that drove him nuts.

But of all the places we visited, the one we ventured to most often was El Monteon. It sits a fair distance from the ocean but it is the gateway to two nice beaches. It is a real Mexican town; a gringo sighting is quite rare other than on the golf course, which is about half a kilometer out of town.

"I think I see someone," Anne had said early one morning, as we stood on the high ridge that overlooks the town of El Monteon and the valley that surrounds it. "But it looks like he's running."

"In this heat," I asked incredulously. Even at this early hour, the air was warm and moist.

This was our third attempt to find the elusive trail from Los Ayala to Lo de Marcos. Unlike back home, you couldn't just look it up on the internet. We had cheated this time; we would not be denied.

The first time we had tried to go on our own, but the trail had ended in a field where cows, horses and, most importantly, bulls were grazing freely. There was a group of Nord Americanos who made the trek each week so we joined them for our second try. It had turned out that we had been on the right trail; you just had to somehow ignore the bulls. The problem was that the group was speed walkers and we were only able to keep up with the few stragglers who thought 'walk' meant exactly that. By El Monteon, we had lost the rest of the group altogether.

So this morning, we had taken the bus to El Monteon, hoping that with an 11 km head start, there was at least some hope that we would be able to keep up.

Like a relay runner getting a running start to ensure the smooth passing of the baton, we started walking. Despite having jogged the 11 kms from Los Ayala to here in less than an hour, the group leader left us literally in his dust in about 10 minutes. So when we took a wrong turn trying to get as far ahead of the rest of the group as we could, and got by-passed by the others, we feared it was back to the drawing board.

And so, here we stood on the peak of the mountain, tired and disappointed. A long stretch of deserted beach stood before us. Four old worn palapas stood at the near end and there was a small sheltered cove at the other.

"We've been here before," I said. "Remember?"

"We biked here one Sunday. On the trail on the far side of the highway. We had to share the path with the donkeys. It ran past the town dump and that small pool next door that a hundred vultures called home. Talk about a vulture paradise: trash and water."

Anne continued to scan the beach.

"That Mexican family sat right there under one of those palapas. They fresh fish and tortillas and kept staring at us. Didn't see many gringos here"

I knew I was babbling but I was frustrated and exhausted and it was better than admitting that we'd lost the trail again.

"And that young girl played Hangman with us in the sand. We were trying out new Spanish words. There must have been what - eight kids. Six of them less than the age of nine. Although that young one was more interested in showing us the dead fish he had found than the game."

"There they are," Anne shouted, interrupting my monologue, as she pointed to a half dozen tiny figures at the end of the beach.

They were gone by the time we had scrambled down the side of the mountain but we tracked their footprints and made it to Lo de Marcos.

"It can't be right," I said as we waited on the side of the road for the collectivo back to Guayabitos. We had walked the last bit on the highway.

It was two more weeks and two more attempts, including one starting from Lo de Marcos and working backwards, before we finally got it right: all 22 kms of it. In hindsight, that should not have been a surprise. 'Trail' certainly overstates the case. In parts, it's cobblestone street, dirt road, foot path, dried-up river-bed, beach and open field. You have to go over, under or through a barb-wire fence in about a dozen places and open half a dozen gates. And then there are the two mountains and two deserted beaches.

It was late March by the time we had finally figured it out, and visited all the towns we figured were worth seeing. The end of our time in Guayabitos was quickly approaching.

"I guess we should decide about next year," I said as we sat on the deck one warm and cloudless night, drinking margaritas and watching the stars twinkle far up over the mountains.

"Let's see: things to do and see, value, weather, friendly people." Anne listed off what was important to her.

My list was not all that different.

"It's a nice beach and there's golf and hiking but it's pretty quiet at night," she began haltingly, clearly unconvinced by her own arguments.

"There's E&R's and Jamie and Hinde's and Soley's," I countered. I knew that the last one would catch her attention: An Italian restaurant in Mexico, run by a fellow from Argentina, that served the best manicotti this side of Little Italy.

"And the Piña Loca," Anne added getting into the spirit.

I didn't need to add that, some nights, the entertainment even came to us. Like the night we were watching TV when we heard some crackling noises outside. They had set the vacant lot next door on fire. We had watched them clearing the lot that afternoon: cutting the trees down with a machete; piling everything in the middle, garbage and all, setting it ablaze and then just going home. As we watched the flames shoot twenty-five feet in the air, inches from the apartment, we thought about calling the Fire Department, but then how do you e-mail 911.

She didn't waste her breath on an argument on value.

Prices for anything that was grown locally were ridiculously cheap; we had often left fruit and vegetable stand with two full bags of produce for $3-$4. A wonderful fresh flower arrangement at the local florist goes for $4-$5. The same went for anything that is labour-intensive. A haircut was $4 and shoe repairs cost less than $2. A doctor's visit might set you back $20 and a dentist's $23. A night out at a Jamie and Hinde's, the gringo bar where you found out what was going on in town, drank cheap beer and listened to the Redneck Mothers, might cost $20, including taxis there and back

The weather was likewise a lost cause. We'd had fifteen minutes of rain in four and a half months.

But it was the people who had stood out most of all that winter. We had met dozens of wonderful new friends. People who came back year after year. Kenny and Laura – great landlords as well as good friends. Our neighbours Pat and Bruce who knew all about the 'Fred Flintstone House'. Roberto the butcher and Sergio the Postmaster. Carol and Frank, who had feasted on the Jambalaya that was the object of that day's scavenger hunt. And Rosalie and Eddie who had driven us home on our first night out on the town, and made us feel welcome.

"I guess we should see Kenny tomorrow," she said. "And see what he has available for next winter.

Thailand and Australia and Florida could wait one more year.

8.
A HERO'S WELCOME

The Emergency Vehicle at Barranca de Huetitan

The adoring fans were lined up five deep along the side of the street as our mini-van edged its way down the avenue. They shouted and waved and sang.

Cheers rang out as I hung my shirt out the window. A hundred car horns honked, adding to the delirious cacophony.

We heard on the radio later that night that a hundred thousand people had flocked to downtown Guadalajara that afternoon to welcome their heroes.

"We might as well enjoy it," Anne said. "Good thing we're not in a rush."

I guess we should have known something was up when there was a TV in every stall of the Guadalajara market. And when every vendor craned their neck to see around us as we wandered through it.

It should have been a clue when the place erupted with a roar so loud that the foundations of the building literally shook.

Las Chivas from Guadalajara, which literally means 'The Goats', are the most popular soccer team in Mexico. They are the only team that refuses to employ any player who is not a Mexican national. It was just happenstance that the tour we had decided to take to the historic center of Guadalajara coincided with the national soccer final. It was just luck that Las Chivas had won. They are like the Maple Leafs of Mexico, except they actually win once in a while. This was there second title in the last 36 years.

Soccer is not a sport here but a religion.

In a perverse way, the scene on that day had made what we had seen the day before make perhaps an inkling of sense. We had seen a lady buying a dozen live chicks at the market. The vendor had carefully placed them in a plastic grocery bag for the woman to take home. But these were not ordinary chicks; they had miniature baseball caps with the Chivas emblem glued to their heads.

I was probably for some sort of pre-game ritual, the details of which we were probably best not to know. And we just thought she was crazier than a bag of chickens.

I wasn't quite sure how we had ended up in the middle of the parade but it seemed only fitting that I bought a shirt through the window of the bus to commemorate the occasion. I waved it frantically to the cheers of the crowd. At least the shirt would easier to pack than a chicken.

I also wasn't quite certain how the driver managed to work his way through the throng of people and back onto the highway to Chapala.

Since this would undoubtedly be our last winter in Mexico in a while, Anne and I had decided to spend a month and a half in the Lake Chapala area before we headed back to Jaltemba Bay.

"There are about 10,000 Canadians and Americans who live in the Lake Chapala area, most of them permanently," we had read in our guidebook. "There are a number of communities that sit along the shores of Lake Chapala, the largest lake in Mexico. It has the second best year-round climate in the world after Nigeria. Lake Chapala is about 45 minutes from Guadalajara, a city of seven million."

All in all, it seemed like a nice change of pace from Jaltemba Bay.

As we made our final arrangements before leaving Canada to head south, I couldn't help but think that while we had gotten good mileage in 'Ou Mexican Jounal' at the expense of the Mexican bureaucracy, there are many good examples, much closer to home, of rules that make little sense. Take Canada Post.

"I want to make sure I have this right," I had said in exasperation to the poor clerk. "If we continue to get our mail delivered like usual, and let it pile up in our mailbox, it would cost nothing. If we get it sent to another address, it would cost $52. But if we ask you to not do anything – don't deliver it, just put it in a cardboard box at the Post Office – it costs $112."

By the way, we also had to pay $50 to Bell Canada to not provide you phone service and a similar amount to our internet provider to not provide internet. I was expecting the garbage men to drop by when they found out we were leaving to ask for money to not pick up our garbage.

As I was paying our final bills and packing for the trip south, the thought crossed my mind that I may have stumbled upon a good way to make some extra money to supplement our retirement income: this idea of getting people to pay you to not do things. All I needed to do was line up half a dozen of our neighbours to agree that I won't deliver their mail to them either and I could send in an invoice to Canada Post for $600.

Whoever said that getting there is half the fun has obviously never traveled through Mexico City. We were, in some ways, the authors of our own misfortune. Not only had we arranged to change planes in the city of twenty million but our booking required a change in airlines: Air Canada from Toronto to Mexico City and Mexicana from there to Guadalajara. That, of course, meant having to retrieve our baggage and check back in.

"It's a Mexicana Flight," I noted, studying the tickets as I struggled with our far-too-many carry-on bags.

"The Mexicana check-in desk is that way," Anne replied, pointing to the far end of the terminal.

"No," the attendant replied solemnly an hour later, as we finally snaked our way to the front of the line. "Esta flight es para Aero Mexico."

"Internationale." he added, indicating the hall to the right.

This seemed to us akin to United operating a Continental flight. And my grade eight geography suggested that a flight from Mexico City to Guadalajara would qualify as a 'Domestic' flight. Anne and I shrugged; who were we to argue with the expert. I decided later that it was our pale white faces that had convinced him.

"Mexico a Guadalajara," the next attendant said, another hour having flown by. He smiled sympathetically at the confused gringos. "Es domestic."

He pronounced the words with an irritating firmness.

'Gate B' was all the board said, except there were 36 Gate B's. It is, I am told, a security rule that the actual gate can't be announced until a half hour before the flight and at the duly-appointed time, they announced B-9 and off we headed. We arrived just in time to see the attendant close the gate as he watched about five people racing desperately towards it. It didn't matter anyway; that flight wasn't going to Puerto Vallarta. Our gate had changed, but they just weren't telling anyone. I'm not sure how we found the right gate, at the other end of the airport, but it was fifteen minutes before takeoff. Luckily, we had left three hours between flights.

As we settled back into our seats, exhausted, I replayed in my head the take-off announcements that I had heard a million times in English, taking my clues from the odd word I knew or could make an educated guess at in the Spanish instructions: 'teléfono celular', 'sistema de navegación' 'presión de aire'. And I wondered, as I often do, is it really true that cell phones interfere with their navigational systems and that if the guy in seat 3B forgot to turn off his phone and gets a call, we are all suddenly going to be hurtling to our deaths in the middle of the Sierra Madre Mountains.

The duplex that we have rented in Chapala turned out to be huge: two bedrooms, a living room as well as a sitting area, one and a half baths and a rooftop balcony that was large enough to play basketball on. It also had a unique Mexican design feature: an open courtyard, complete with a fountain, between the living room and the bedrooms. It was this particular feature that alerted us to the first major difference between here and Guayabitos: the temperature. It got chilly when the sun went down. It was cold enough that we could still see our breath, even when we wrapped ourselves in blankets and lit up the fireplace, as we watched TV in the living room. I guess the fireplace should have tipped us off. That or the young lady manning the internet café who was bundled up in a parka so thick she looked like the Michelin Man.

The unit came with something else that we hadn't anticipated: a maid. Ramona was a hard worker but painfully shy.

"Her husband is in prison," our landlord Tony has advised us. "So she can use the extra money."

"It's lovely," Anne told her as she surprised us on Christmas Eve with a framed picture.

Ramona smiled sweetly.

"Did you do this?" I asked.

"No, No," she replied, "my husband make."

It was at that moment that a myth was shattered. I had pictured a Mexican Penitentiary as a hard place. Tough hombres breaking rocks with picks or lifting weights in a crowded prison yard. But now my vision was quite different. I imagined tough cartel members, the bulging muscles on their arms resplendent with tattoos, sitting around a table with blunt scissors, construction paper and a paint brush, doing arts and crafts.

If the duplex was a pleasant surprise, Lake Chapala itself was anything but.

"Do you think anyone swims in there?" Anne asked, as we stared in the black-green foul smelling mess that was Lake Chapala.

"Not without a wet suit. No, make that two wet suits," I replied as we watched a snake slither through the slime. "And a double dose of hepatitis vaccine."

There are hot springs just up the road. They have three pools, some of which reach 105 degrees, and a natural steam bath built into a cave. We did all of our swimming there.

If we were looking for a change of pace from Jaltemba Bay, we certainly found it. The area is quite modern and Americanized; you can survive quite well here without speaking a word of Spanish and, indeed, many of the gringos here even seem to take some perverse pride in the fact that they can't speak any of the language. Most Nord Americanos live in gated communities here and pretend that they are not really in Mexico.

The Lake Chapala Society organizes monthly tour to restaurants in Guadalajara and has an English language library. There's a store that specializes in selling all kinds of imported food, although we did have to take out a second mortgage so that Anne could buy herself some kind of cereal that at least looks like Shreddies. There is actually a paved bike path that runs the length of the lake. There's an Animal Shelter and an English little theatre group that has built its own playhouse. Art galleries and fine dining restaurants abound and unlike Guayabitos, beef is quite plentiful here. We even saw one restaurant advertising Chihuahua steaks, which is quite surprising as I didn't think there would be that much meat on the little guys.

There are five major towns along the lake: Chapala, Ajijic - which is the real gringo hub - San Antonio, St Juan de Cosalo and Jocotepec. And an hour's bus ride takes you to the town of Mazamitla, which is a perfect replica of a Swiss Mountain village. But for us, the main attraction was probably Guadalajara.

There was the historic downtown of Guadalajara: the Cathedral, the Teatro Degollado, the Cultural Centre. The haunting murals of Jose Orozco that adorn many of the public buildings serve as a tool for teaching the country's history to a nation with a high rate of illiteracy. Mariachi bands compete for attention in the Plaza Tapatia.

Barranca de Huetitan is a canyon that sits literally on the edge of Guadalajara. It's a five mile hike down into the canyon and five miles straight back up, with crosses along the way where people have died, presumably of a heart attack. It's much safer now; there was a donkey tied up about three-quarters of the way down: the emergency vehicle for people who can't make it back up.

We toured Tlaquepaque where we dined on the national dish in a sidewalk café: stuffed peppers with an almond sauce; red, green and white; the colours of the Mexican flag. The streets are lined with fine galleries and shops, where they sell abstract sculptures of pigs with wings and zebras with lion's heads. Artwork which suggested that the artists were ingesting something much stronger than the weed that was the source of that sickly sweet smell back at that little hovel by Alta Vista.

Tonala is the craft centre of the country. Our tour stopped at a paper mache factory where they make everything from birds and zebras to life-size nativity figures. There was a visit to a potter's studio. He has exhibited around the world and has even had a book published of his work, but you had to walk through his house to get to the studio. The guide explained that he shined and finished his work with fool's gold, and we bought a hand-designed plate for twenty bucks. But it was our tour of the glass blowing factory that was most vivid in my mind.

"Workers' Compensation would have had a fit," I whispered.

Workers dashed everywhere, crisscrossing each other, holding six foot poles with molten glass burning on the ends. Not only did they not have any safety equipment on, most of them weren't even wearing shirts.

But then speaking of lax standards, we saw an ad posted on a lamp post one day: 'Single busy businessman looking for someone to cook for him; must be 18-30, female and attractive'. Try running something like that in Canada.

It was New Year's Day when we boarded the first class bus back to Jaltemba Bay. We had stayed an extra day. As we rode down the highway, I thought of our friends Terry and Carmen. The journal had convinced them to come down for two months and they had rented the place next to us.

I imagined Laura, our landlord's better half, driving them from the airport along the dark winding roads. I pictured their faces as a tour bus full of families from Guadalajara carted their belongings into the apartment that Terry and Carmen had thought was to be our place for the winter. I could see them with that 'what the hell have we done' look as loud pounding music echoed from the place next door until early the next day. And I remembered Anne and me, a year earlier, feeling much the same way.

It was early the next morning, on our first day back in Jaltemba Bay, when we wandered down Avenida del Sol Nuevo in Guayabitos to see what had changed in the last six months. Roberto the butcher and Sergio the Postmaster and the gentleman who runs the Internet Café, whose name I am ashamed to admit that I hadn't learned, all came out to warmly greet us, to shake our hands and to welcome us back to town. It truly felt like a hero's welcome. Except this time, it really was meant for us.

9.
DIGGING A WELL ON THE 'OTHER' SIDE OF THE BRIDGE

I remember distinctly when Anne and I first set foot in La Peñita de Jaltemba. It was the Thursday of the first week of our first year in Guayabitos.

Thursday is market day and La Peñita has the biggest market in the State of Nayarit. In fact, for all intents and purposes, it has two markets.

The 'gringo' market fills the town plaza. Vendors come from all over the country to sell blankets and table cloths and handcrafted jewellery. It is here you buy the distinctive blue goblets and jugs and water glasses that we had seen being made at that glass blowing plant we had visited in Guadalajara that was an accident waiting to happen. Native women from up in the mountains sit behind tables laden with plates and bowls decorated with brightly painted chilli peppers or scenes of donkeys or mountains or Mexicans with big sombreros sleeping in the shade of a cactus. And everything is "almost free".

There is a saying in Mexico that when you see something, you want, buy it or you may never see it again. It is never truer than at the market.

But it is not just souvenirs that are for sale. The smell of churros, the fried dough snack that is the Mexican equivalent of a donut, assaults the nostrils as they cook in a bubbling vat of oil.

A middle-aged woman hands out samples of peanut brittle and tempts you with the aroma of fresh ground coffee. Newbies, still too timid to buy directly from the fishermen, buy shrimp from the lady with the umbrella, the umbrella designed to ensure that there is at least some ice remaining under them until the close of the market. Nord Americanos dine on omelettes at Soleys, the Italian restaurant that sits across from the plaza and fight with the locals for a place in line at the vegetable stand, the one that serves as the border between the 'gringo' market and the Mexican one.

The 'other' market runs south for five blocks from the plaza to Lucio Blanco. A vendor displays an eclectic collection of rusted out tools and motor parts on a blanket. You can but fresh pineapple or papaya or watermelon in a plastic cup. An open grill cooks tacos with a meat of some description that assaults the nostrils in quite a different manner than the churros that cook on the plaza. Salsa music blares from overworked ghetto blasters as CD merchants compete for business. Sellers hawk DVDs of the latest Hollywood movies – English with Spanish sub-titles – available well before they hit the legitimate market and although the quality is generally pretty good, there is an occasional break in the action when the fellow in the row ahead gets up to go for popcorn. Everything is for sale: used cloths, birdhouses, Tupperware, cancer remedies, stuffed toys, hand-made furniture.

It may be only a hundred meters or so across the bridge that joins Guayabitos and La Peñita but, in many ways, the communities are worlds apart; the difference is as great as the gap between the two La Peñita markets.

The bridge itself has an interesting history. The highway between the two towns is busy day and night; as the people who live in La Peñita make their way to and from their jobs in Guayabitos.

There is a so much traffic , in fact, that a couple of years ago they built the pedestrian suspension bridge between the two communities to allow people to walk between them without having to venture out onto the highway. They call it the 'Bridge of Life'. The small crosses and flowers that appear along the sides of the highway mark the places where less fortunate souls failed to survive the trip before the bridge was built.

The plaza in Guayabitos sits empty most of the time; the La Peñita plaza teems with life. Children kick around a soccer ball in the afternoon and old men sit in the shade. A young woman in a wheelchair sells used clothing and household items and a stand serves birria: goat stew.

In Guayabitos, the plaza entertainment might be a classical string quartet from Tepic or a dance troupe from Puerto Vallarta. The only entertainment in the La Peñita square is the carnival.

Every holiday weekend, which seemed to occur pretty much every week, we would awake to see a hustle and bustle around the square. The kiddy rides were similar to the ones one would see at any small town fair up north. There was usually one of those inflatable castles that kids bounce around in that has always seemed to me like a lawsuit in waiting. But then there was also a booth that served liquor and games that were quite different than those we were used to. There was the 'toss darts at a wheel' game that Anne played one night and walked away with a flask size bottle of tequila and a beer. Unfortunately, it wasn't the quart-size bottle of beer which, for some reason, they refer to as 'family' size. The term always made me imagine some señora calling out to her husband: "Why don't you take the kids to the beach and pick up a couple of family size beers for them on the way."

But our favourite was the Mexican equivalent of the 'knock over the milk cans with a softball' game. In this version, you throw a good size rock at a target of empty beer bottles and if you break three you win a six-pack of beer. Broken glass from past winners crunches beneath the feet of both players and spectators.

And then there are the parades. The biggest parade we saw in Guayabitos was on what we assumed must be National Junky Car Day and featured souped-up Volkswagen Beetles and GEO Metros. A thousand people lined the streets to watch Volkswagens roaring down the street shooting flames out of their exhausts. La Peñita parades have a more family feel. The Mardi Gras Parade featured marching bands and students from the local schools dressed in colourful outfits, riding in the back of pick-ups, as beaming parents looked on. And a clean-up effort beforehand, where they hauled all the non-working vehicles off the avenida.

Stores in Guayabitos stock imported goods and tourist-friendly sizes. Shops on the other side of the bridge feature 'jumbo-sized' items like a two kg size can of tuna or a litre bottle of Worcestershire Sauce, to meet the needs of the large Mexican families. But there was nothing that could match the bag of Cheese Puffs we stumbled across one day that was taller than Anne.

It really was a tale of two cities.

But not only do I remember the first time we set foot in La Peñita, I also remember the first words that I said to Anne that day. "Who the heck would ever live here?"

The streets were dusty. The houses run down. And the shady looking young men, who stood on the corner as we passed by, eyed us warily.

The 'who' turned out to be Anne and I.

"What about next year?" we had asked our landlord Kenny at the end of the previous winter season.

"Well," he had stammered and we knew that the rest of the answer was not going to be good. "If you stay where you are, I'm afraid I'll have to double your rent."

We knew Guayabitos was growing more popular and, probably, more expensive, now that it fell within 'Riviera Nayarit', the new tourist destination that the Mexican Government was working hard to promote.

"But I do have a place in La Peñita," Kenny had added hopefully. "And I can let you have it next year for the same price as you're paying now."

La Peñita had grown on us a little since those first impressions were formed. Every Thursday, we had come to join the long line of winter visitors who made the trek there for the market. We biked there often to shop on the avenida at real stores: the hardware store, the magazine shop or the bakery, since almost every store in Guayabitos seemed to be either a supermercado, a pharmacia or, most common of all, a souvenir shop.

The Pacifico Bus Terminal was in La Peñita and experience had taught us that it was a lot easier to buy a ticket to PV there and wait for the bus than to stand on the highway in Guayabitos and play the 'guess which bus stops and which one is express' game. Besides there was even a washroom at the terminal, even if it did cost two pesos, which was no small convenience, given the advisability of a quick pit stop before the long and sometimes bumpy trip to PV.

Besides, 'price' was high on our list of reasons to come here and half price was, after all, half price.

"I'm having a well dug there tomorrow," Kenny added. "Why don't you come over and have a look."

He didn't bother to add the reason for the new well. Since no-one in town bothered to pay their water bills, the water company didn't have enough money to pay for the electricity to run the pump at the town well. Therefore, there was rarely any water running through the pipes that ran underneath the town and fed the homes and businesses. And since no-one received any water they didn't bother to pay their bills.

Kenny could have told us that the old Santa Ana Hotel sat at the corner of Amado Nervo and Salina Cruz, but this bit of information would not have proved particularly useful since, other than the occasional hand-lettered sign on the wall of a house, the majority of the streets in town had no signs. And it wasn't possible to give us a street address, as the building had no number; Kenny had yet to purchase one from the municipal authorities in Compostelo. Besides, when numbers frequently go '14, 26, 118, 8' as you proceed up the street, this would have been of little help either; I can only assume that the numbers reflect the order in which people purchased then rather than the location of the building on the street.

So, instead, Kenny had given us some directions that actually made sense: "It's one block from the ocean and one block north of the estuary that runs between Guayabitos and La Peñita".

It was a two storey cream coloured building that occupied half a city block. The wall was punctuated by a series of large red steel doors that each marked what had once been a hotel room. Above the door at the far end, 'Officina' was carefully lettered in black paint. The stairs that led up to the second floor were open to the street. A narrow walkway led to a series of more doors and a huge patio at the end. A series of ornamental balusters, painted bright red to match the doors, gave it a real old Mexican flavour. The patio was partly covered by a battered old palapa that hung limply from the roof and had clearly outlasted its life expectancy by about two rainy seasons.

We recognized the building at once.

"Kenny took us here that first day, when he gave us the ten pesos tour," Anne said, before adding "didn't he?"

I nodded yes, but decided not to reminder her of the reason. Kenny had stopped to replace a couple of the light bulbs that lit the stairs to the second floor because "the crack heads are always stealing them to light joints."

Since we knew Kenny owned the place and, as far as we knew, there were only two tenants in the whole building, we would come here sometimes at sunset. There was a top deck you could reach after a couple of very tight winding steel staircases. We would bring along a couple of Coronas. The sun would set just past the point of land that separated Guayabitos from Los Ayala to the south. The red would slowly seep across the sky to the small island that guards the entrance to Jaltemba Bay. The mountains that hugged the towns to the sea loomed behind us.

The apartment itself had two bedrooms and two full bathroom, although the later were somewhat worse for wear. In contrast to greens and oranges and yellows of our first year's accommodations, everything here was white. The widows had bars and screens but no glass. When a car drove by at night, you would swear that it driving right into the living room; and the night of our annual fifteen minutes of rain, every time a truck drove through the puddles, it felt like you were going to get splashed as you sat on the couch. But the best feature was the huge patio, which we found out later had served as a restaurant in the building's previous incarnation as a hotel.

"I just have to check on the well," Kenny said, as he completed the tour.

It took a moment to register as the lack of any visible equipment had meant that we had completely forgotten about Kenny's other reason for being there.

Kenny opened the door to the 'Officina' and, as we looked inside, we both stood there with that 'deer in the headlights' look. Two workers stood in the office, sweat pouring down their brows as, shovels in hand, they dug feverously through the floor of the building. Digging a well.

I'm still not sure what had sold Anne: the price or the patio or the sunsets. But, whatever the reason, we had booked the place for our second season before we left that day.

Family Size Cheetos

10.
BRING BACK MY BABY TO ME

I rode my bike to school all that second year. It was just like being back in the seventh grade, except back then I didn't have to worry about whether bicycles or donkeys had the right of way.

We had bought ourselves bikes from the bike shop in La Peñita. They weren't great but they only cost a hundred dollars each. We had been smart enough the second year to bring along good padded biking shorts. The roads could be a pain – literally.

"I want to be able to at least carry on a basic conversation in Spanish by the end of this winter," I had announced at the start of our second season.

"What was it?" Anne had asked. "Don't you want to be like all those folks in Ajijic who are proud that they can't speak a word of Spanish."

"Maybe. Or maybe I'm just tired of charades and of ordering what I understand from the menu, rather than what I actually want to eat. Or of having to bring the damn digital camera into the hardware store to show him pictures of what we want."

And so, three days a week I got out the bike and headed off to class.

I had learned the basic rule of language training during my working life, when the Federal Government had sent me off to learn

French: vocabulary trumps truth. It didn't matter whether I had stumbled upon the cure for cancer the night before, or rescued two young children from drowning in the Pacific Ocean and received the Mexican Medal of Honour, when the teacher asked "What did you do yesterday?", the answer was invariably: "I went to the beach" or "I read a book" or "I watched television." Those things I knew how to say.

Well, actually, I didn't learn the past tense until late in the year, so I actually answered "I am going to the beach yesterday", but that was close enough.

Sofia was our instructor. She was a striking young señorita with a penchant for choosing the wrong men. It was something she reminded us of when she started out most lessons with a story about her date from the previous night and the disaster that it had turned into.

We learned a lot about Sofia's life over the course of the winter.

"My parents were together for thirty or more years but didn't get married until they were sixty-five. I think it has something to do with Social Security."

It struck us all as odd for a country that is so devoutly Catholic.

"I teach English to the students at the kinders in La Peñita. There are four hundred kids in the kinders in town."

That seemed like a lot of kindergarten students for a town that might have a population of ten thousand or so. And not all the kids go to school here; they put some of them out to work early. We've seen kids three or four years old selling stuff on the beach and children about ten serving drinks at one of the local bars. I guess that there are some rules of the Catholic Church that are adhered to more closely than others.

But, as they say, people who live in glass houses shouldn't throw stones. I must confess that I am not a particularly religious person myself. I could probably name four of the twelve disciples, but after John, Paul, George and Ringo I'd be at a loss.

Class size at Spanish school varied from week to week as people came and went from and to the frozen north. That meant a lot of repetition which, for some of us, was not all that bad a thing. We had as many as nine in the class at one time, but by the end of the year, there was just me: three private one hour lessons a week for ten bucks. And by then, with a smaller audience, Sofia's tales of her love-life woes has stopped.

Some of the lessons in particular proved extremely valuable. I remember taking detailed notes from the class on ordering tacos and was successful from then on in sticking to beef and pork and sausage, while avoiding the intestine, tongue and brain. I could guess now what that smell was coming form the taco vendor in the 'local' end of the market.

We had heard lots of 'bilingual' conversations here, as gringos tried to practice their Spanish, while the locals worked on their English. Things like:

> Gringo: "How do you say 'You're Welcome'?"
> Local: "De nada"
> Gringo: "Ah, gracias."
> Local: "You're welcome."

I had had many such conversations with Roberto the butcher that year. We talked about baseball, the Blue Jays and Niagara Falls; and futbol, Las Chivas and Chichen Itza.

And by the end of the season, I could at least get by. I could form a complete sentence and order what I wanted. And I could say what I did yesterday in the past tense and what I planned to do tomorrow in the future.

But it was not only the language that was confusing; it took a while to get used to the money as well. This became very clear the day Anne felt particularly generous and gave the two young boys packing groceries at the supermercado a noteworthy two dollar tip in pesos, with a strict admonition to make sure that they shared it. Her muttering about their ingratitude stopped quickly once she realized that the gratuity was not two dollars, but twenty cents.

"I hope they didn't spend it all in one place," I had reminded her later.

There was good reason for the confusion. During our first two seasons, we got anywhere between nine and ten pesos to the Canadian dollar, which at least made us feel rich when the ATM slip showed that we had forty thousand in our chequing account.

There was one ATM in La Peñita, just outside the Bancomer Bank, and one in Guyabitos which stood by itself on the side of the street. And other than on market day or Christmas Week or Semana Santa, they generally had money in them. They would generally dispense five hundred peso bills, the ones that most stores were loathe to accept since it meant giving up all their change. It was only on the rare occasion when we were about to make a major purchase that the machine would somehow sense this and dispense a wad of one hundred and two hundred peso notes thick enough to choke a horse or, perhaps more appropriately, a donkey.

And then there were the dreaded torn bills. We'd get them from an ATM or buried deep inside a stack of bills we received as change.

"No," the merchants would all say indicating even a small missing corner or a tiny tear.

"A la Bancomer," they would add, smiling proudly at their powers of observation and pointing to the Bancomer Bank down the street.

Since that would mean an hour's wait to exchange it for a new one, we soon learned to play the game of musical bills, slipping it into another stack of currency and hoping not to be caught holding it when the music stopped.

Coins come in a variety of denominations: 10 pesos, 5 pesos, 2 pesos, 1 peso, 50 centavos, 20 centavos, 10 centavos, 5 centavos and Chicklets. The first three are bimetallic, with either aluminum bronze centers and stainless steel rings, or the reverse.

"They remind me of the quarters that the Canadian Mint put out one year to commemorate Remembrance Day," Anne had noted. "You know. The ones with red poppies that wore off and the centers that fell out."

As for the Chicklets, one night when they ran out of coins, they gave us our change in those one cent packages of gum that you used to get on Halloween.

But, if adapting to the language and currency was problematic, adapting to the culture of the town was more difficult still. Unlike its neighbour Guayabitos to the south, where an evening's entertainment might be comprised of classical string quartets and folkloric dancers, the entertainment enjoyed by the good folks of La Peñita had more of a working class bent: a carnival on the town plaza featuring that throw the boulder at the beer bottle game, the circus, the rodeo and fireworks.

We had learned through the years that Mexicans love their fireworks: not the kind that send a waterfall of colours across the night sky but the kind that just make noise. Lots of noise.

We had heard them in Chapala; every morning at 6:00 AM they would fire off six rockets as a sort of town wake-up call. At first, we thought it was just because the day we arrived was the Festival of the Revolution, which started November 18 and ran to November 30. But that was quickly followed by the Festival of the Virgin of Guadaloupe, which ran from December 1 to December 12 and also featured lots of rockets. It ended just in time for the beginning of Christmas festivities on December 13.

And La Peñita was no different. They fired off rockets to celebrate Christmas and New Years and Easter and, for the benefit of the one Jewish Mexican in town, Hanukah. Explosions echoed off the cement walls to tell us it was someone's birthday or anniversary or wedding day or just the fact that it was Friday.

We had successfully resisted the urge to go to the circus, which set up several times a year across the highway. It wasn't as if we didn't know when it was going on. A fleet of flatbeds driving through town carrying lions and tigers and elephants was sufficient to tip us off, even if my Spanish wasn't yet good enough to catch all the details that the driver called out through a megaphone. In fact, we even saw the parade twice one time when they ran into a water truck standing diagonally across the intersection, two massive tree trunks holding it up where the rear wheels have fallen off, and had to back up and try again.

But the bull ring was just a block and a half from the apartment, so we knew we were going to hear whatever was going on there whether we went or not. We figured we might as well get the video as well as the audio.

Our first rodeo featured a competition between two teams of charros from La Peñita and Compostela. And since we knew Compostela was 'the cowboy city' from an earlier visit there, we figured the local boys would be in tough.

But La Peñita had a secret weapon: Elmundio. We had seen him almost every morning riding from his home across the highway to the bull ring. He sat tall and proud and erect in the saddle with a ten gallon hat and a bright western shirt and a wide moustache that would make Pancho Villa proud. It was clear that he had been on horseback for at least seventy-five of his eighty years.

We expected bull riding or bronco riding or maybe even a barrel race, but what we got was a completely different set of contests. It began with horse sliding. Riders would gallop as fast as they could up to a white line marked in lime across the floor of the ring. The horse would fall on command and slide as far as they could on their ass: the horse's ass that is, they didn't have a donkey partner. I cringed as I imagined a giant sheet of sandpaper being run across my own butt. Elmundio was the star of the show and the local heroes soon had an early lead in the competition.

We watched as the charros from both teams formed a tight line down one side of the arena and wondered what was next.

A terrified stallion burst through the gate with a charro in hot pursuit, attempting to lasso him around the back leg. The contest between the two teams was as tied up as the poor horse by the end of the second event.

We called it a day after the third event: the Mexican equivalent of burger flipping, although the burger was still on the hoof. A charro would ride astride a cow and attempt to grab him by the tail and flip him over on his back. We were a little afraid of what they would come up with next.

While the charro competition was sparsely attended, perhaps with good reason, we knew from the moment we walked in that the bull riding demonstration was the social event of the season. Well, perhaps not from the first moment we walked in.

"Go early. Five O'Clock. Get good seat," our friend Roberto who ran the butcher shop in Guayabitos had advised us.

The same family owned the bull ring and every butcher shop in Jaltemba Bay. It's a Mexican version of vertical integration: to-day's competitors would be tomorrow's ground chuck. When we arrived at the suggested hour, we were the only spectators there besides the beer vendors who, we would later find out, were getting set up for a big night of sales; we figured Roberto might also be getting a cut of liquor profits.

The ring itself was a beehive of activity. Riders stretched their legs, and those of their steeds around the ring. Workers hauled in speaker after speaker, the event having been billed as a concert as well as a rodeo

"Now we know why it always seems like the band is playing in the apartment next to us and not a block and a half down the street,"

I said as they mounted the fourth and, fortunately, final row of speakers.

As the workers built a giant wall of metal gates and tables around the speakers to protect them from any wayward charging bulls, the crowd began slowly to assemble. They arrived in small and, sometimes not so small, groups. Gringos were clearly in the minority. It was a family affair: parents, children, aunts, uncles, grandparents, all decked out in their finest western duds. The kids all looked like miniature replicas of John Wayne or Dale Evans. There was a hint of counterfeit Chanel and Old Spice in the air.

The arena was full by the time the festivities began and the blare of trumpets echoed loudly off the concrete walls as three mariachi bands competed for attention and Miss La Peñita and her four princesses swayed seductively to the beat.

Suddenly, after three or four songs, the gate burst open and a cowboy entered the ring, clutching desperately to a raging bull. The sound of the crowd shouting encouragement to its hero as the bull bucked violently around the ring would, for a moment, almost drown out the music.

And then, accordion and drums and brass would emerge again as the bull grew either tired or bored and began simply walking around the ring. Three or four of the hero's compatriots would lasso the bull and try to coax him back into the stall. The smell of stale beer mingled with the odours one would expect in a bull ring, as the spectators tossed their empty plastic cups into the ring. We didn't know if this was intended as a salute or a sign of disappointment.

There would be three or four more songs. Miss La Peñita and her four princesses would again sway seductively to the beat. And then, it would be time for the next rider.

There was one moment of silence when a rider was knocked unconscious. But the lull was short lived, as eight people ran into the ring to carry him out, arms linked to form a makeshift stretcher. The music has resumed even before they had reached the grandstand.

I'm not sure what resulted in the end of that portion of the night's festivities. Perhaps they ran out of bulls or of riders, the unfortunate accident having caused some would-be participants to decide on a career change. Or perhaps it had become too dangerous to continue amid the growing pile of plastic beer cups in the ring. For whatever reason, it was time for the headliners to take to the stage.

"We must be the only folks here who have no idea who these guys are," I whispered to Anne.

People streamed from the stands to the floor of the arena to get a closer look and to dance among the plastic cups and the cow patties. A giant screen played videos of their hits.

In Canada and the United States we keep our children tethered to us. We street-proof them and make sure they are tightly buckled into their car seats. And that is not a bad thing, with all the threats that they are exposed to. But La Peñita lives in simpler times; it reminds me of how life was back in the fifties when I grew up. Kids still play under the few streetlights that actually work until way into the evening. They build forts out of fridge boxes and surfboards out of hunks of styrofoam. They ride around in the back of pick-up trucks. They don't talk to strangers, but only because there are so few of them in this town; everyone is an aunt or uncle, a cousin, a neighbour, a co-worker.

There were many babes in arms at the show that day. They were wrapped up tightly in blankets to protect them from what, for them, would be the cool evening air. We watched as they passed from mother to aunt to friend to cousin, each person taking their turn to cuddle them and whisper sweet words. Some of the babies seemed to make it half way around the arena.

Fireworks lit the sky as the band played its final encore. They were even the kind of fireworks that you can actually see as well as hear.

"I hope that all those babies ended up in the right hands," Anne said as we headed for the exits under the rainbow of colour that filled the black sky above our heads.

11.
B-B-BARRY'S ON BICYCLES AND TWO FOURS

Some people come to La Peñita de Jaltemba because they are running to something: great weather, a nice beach, excellent prices and good friends. Others obviously come to run away from something.

If there was ever a good example of the latter, it was Kirk Swaggerty.

'Most Wanted Fugitive Captured in La Peñita' screamed the headline in the Jaltemba Sol, our on-line newspaper. We had come to learn that many of the articles in Jaltemba Sol revolve around various drinking and social events. So, like almost everyone else, I at first assumed that the story had something to do with the band that billed themselves as 'Most Wanted' and played once a week at Jaimie and Hinde's Bar. I couldn't for the life of me figure out why someone would be 'fleeing' them, and why they would be subsequently 'captured' if they were. The truth turned out to be something far more sinister.

Kirk Swaggerty was at the top of the Most Wanted list put out by the Illinois Department of Corrections. He had warrants for homicide and home invasion. And here he was in little old La Peñita. There was a picture of him under the headline sitting at the bar at Jaimie and Hinde's, drinking a beer with his friends, not looking all that different from the wanted picture juxtaposed next to it, other than the ball cap pulled down tightly on his head. It turned out he had been living here for a while and had even adopted a dog from the Jaltemba Bay Animal Rescue Spay and Neuter clinic. I guess there really is nowhere you can hide, especially when you don't bother to keep your face out of the paper.

There were all kinds of characters in La Peñita. Some of them were running from something much less serious

There were what Anne and I liked to call "B-B-Barrys". We had met their namesake several years earlier while we were spending a couple of weeks in Puerto Vallarta on vacation.

At first we had thought it was a misprint when we saw the brochure: B-B-Barry's B-B-Bikes. Anne and I had decided to rent some bikes for the day to get some exercise.

"B-b-bikes?" he had stuttered as we entered the tiny shop nestled between a jewellery store and a paint store on a back street. This was a man who was clearly comfortable in his own skin.

What was most memorable about the day was not the trip up and down the foothills on the outskirts of town that ended in a wonderful secluded spring. It was not the fact that one of the pedals fell off Anne's bike as she hurtled helplessly down the steep slope on the way back to town. It wasn't even the fact that, by some strange quirk of fate – or at least we thought it to be so – there was a young man with a full set of box wrenches sitting on the sidewalk at the bottom of the sharp incline, grateful for the pesos we gave him to help put the pedal back on. No, what was most memorable was B-B-Barry himself.

He was a tall, thin character with an infectious smile and long hair tied back in a pony tail. It was clear that he loved what he did. And, while we dared not ask, we certainly left the shop with the impression that the sixties had been very good to B-B-Barry.

'B-B-Barry' became our little code word when we saw someone our age who's demeanour belied the fact that they knew all the words to 'Stairway to Heaven'. That they had been to Woodstock, or at least had seen the movie half a dozen times. And that they had experienced the subtle pleasure of sitting on a bean bag chair for hours admiring the intricate manoeuvrings of a lava lamp.

La Peñita certainly had its share of 'B-B-Barrys'.

Drugs are the elephant in the room in La Peñita. You know they are there; the sweet smell would drift up to our balcony on occasion as groups of young locals wandered past on their way to the beach. You would sometimes catch a whiff as you walked home from the town plaza late at night. You would see people sometimes tittering away at things that would certainly not merit that level of amusement. But, we had never seen people smoking in the open or had someone approach us with goods for sale. It was certainly not like Jamaica where beach vendors openly toked doobies as long and thick as a rolled up wall poster.

But then maybe we just didn't look the type, as an earlier trip to Amsterdam had driven home.

"We really don't sell coffee here," the little piss-ant of a young man had whispered discretely to us as we had trundled up to the bar in one of the city's infamous 'Coffee Shops' many years earlier. The voice reminded me of a little old grandmother admonishing her granddaughter that "you don't wear white after Labour Day."

I was no prude in these matters. It had been some time, but I had certainly 'indulged' in my university days. After all, it took me until two years after graduation to realize that 'Stoned Wheat Thins' got their name not from the fact that were an excellent antidote for the munchies but from the ingredient that gave the crackers their unique flavour.

"Two 'brownies' to go," we ordered with a smirk just to spite him.

The brownies did give us a unique perspective for our visit to the famous Van Gogh Museum where we drew stern looks from the staff and fellow tourists alike as we giggled our way through the section of the museum dedicated to the artist's 'Mr Potato Head' years.

While it would be foolhardy to downplay the negative effects of drugs on Mexico, the romanticization of drugs and the drug cartels, for which the country is so roundly criticized, is certainly not unique to this part of the world.

There is a whole grocery store chain in the States, Trader Joe's, that certainly seems to be solely designed to meet the late night munchie needs of those who partake. They sell tofu and goat cheese burgers, chocolate crisps, smoked salmon and spinach filled crepes and seriously seedy and nutty wafers, but don't stock instant coffee.

There is a museum in Jackson, Tennessee dedicated to the memory of Casey Jones whose claim to fame, if you believe the Grateful Dead's version of events, was driving a train high on cocaine and slamming it into the back of a stalled freight train.

And even as far back as ancient times, the Greeks worshiped the priestess of the oracle at Delphi.

"She would chew on laurel leaves, go into a trance and begin raving, with her ravings being 'translated' by the priests of the temple into elegant hexameters," our tour guide had explained to us.

"Great gig," I whispered to Anne. "If the answers were right, she was a hero and if the pronouncements proved false, it was the fault of the priests who must have got it wrong."

"One of her most famous warnings, one which had won a great battle," she continued "was heard by the priests as build a wall of wooden ships."

"Depends how bad those laurel leaves tasted," I said later on the bus. "Maybe what she really said was what the hell is this shit."

But the real drug of choice in La Peñita was alcohol. There were certainly lots of drinkers, and plenty of opportunities to do so.

Every Wednesday is rib night at Matejas. And each Thursday, Most Wanted, the band not Kirk Swaggerty, plays at Jaimie and Hinde's. On Friday, you can go to the Bavarian Gardens to hear the Perez Brothers sing Beach Boy tunes with a Spanish accent. And then there is the beach party every Sunday at Matejas where you can dance on a table for a free T-shirt. And every day, of course, has a Happy Hour somewhere and there is always a house party some place.

It is not a town for the faint of liver.

And then there were the two kinds of angels: the kind like our friend Carol who help out at the spay and neuter clinics and end up taking home all the strays that no-one else will adopt. And the kind that the Rolling Stones hired as 'security' at Altamont.

We had been invited one afternoon to a birthday party at a hacienda right on the beach. The thing that had struck us was that, for some reason, many of the guests were retired bikers, including one who introduced himself as the retired president of the Toronto Chapter of the Vagabonds.

"So what kind of pension plan do you figure the Vagabonds have?" I had whispered to Anne.

He looked the part: sleeveless shirt, two armfuls of tattoos. He wore a leather vest, the Vagabonds emblem proudly visible, in spite of the oppressive heat. Mind you, he had a lot less hair and more belly than he probably had in his glory days. He looked no more than fifty-five.

"Maybe he got some kind of early-retirement package from the Club," Anne replied. "Reduced pension and any two hits of his choosing. After all, the Asian gangs were starting to move in. Maybe the Vagabonds were looking to lay off some staff so they offered a buyout instead."

And, finally, there were the 'Uncle Jose Gringos'. Like the title character in Uncle Tom's Cabin, they are the gringos who are working so hard to be what they're not that they try to out-Mexican the Mexicans.

"Why don't you join us," the gentleman at the next table asked one night as we finished the last of our meal at a restaurant. Anne and I sat at one table and he and his wife sat at another. We were the last four patrons.

"We live in El Monteon," he offered as we moved to his table and my suspicions were immediately aroused. There were very few Nord Americanos who lived there.

"We really like it there," he noted, before adding with a conspiratorial whisper, "there aren't that many gringos where we live. All of our friends are Mexican."

"We are very good friends with our Mexican neighbours," his wife chirped in as her eyes surveyed the parking lot for any of those other 'offending' gringos. I wondered why they had latched on to us. Maybe it was because I was wearing a La Peñita T-shirt and not one from Jaimie and Hinde's or Matejas, or one of the other bars where the gringos tend to hang out.

I have great admiration for Nord Americanos who work hard to learn the language and get to know their Mexican neighbours. We had ourselves acquired a small core of Mexican friends: Roberto the butcher and Victor at the bicycle shop and Jose from Guadalajara who lived next door to us; they happily struggled to comprehend my pigeon Spanish. But 'Uncle Jose Gringos' tended to learn the language and make friends with their neighbours for the sole purpose of differentiating themselves from the rest of us.

They like to brag that they are not 'like the other gringos'. They say things like "I prefer to go the beach on days when there are only Mexican there because gringos are too rowdy", a statement that would make even a local laugh. Mexicans understand that they have a vibrant and loud culture.

As we bid adieu to our new friends, the irony could not help but strike me. They had spent the evening trying to impress upon us how much like the Mexicans they were, all the while drinking riesling and eating jaeger schnitzel in the Bavarian Gardens German restaurant. If this had been Berlin, I'm sure they would have told us that "they preferred to eat in a restaurant with all Germans because the Americans were just too punctual."

12.

THE TWO WEEK OVERNIGHT COURIER

He was a rotund man with a thick moustache and he greeted his clients with warm hugs and firm handshakes as he worked the waiting room like a politician in full campaign mode.

"His first cousin is the Minister of Finance," our landlord Kenny had whispered to us; politics was clearly in the Señor's blood.

But I knew that Kenny had provided this little tidbit of information not to explain our host's need to shake every hand and kiss every baby, but to let us know that the man had connections and would be able to expedite our transaction.

Expeditious is the last word that would have come to mind as I recalled the events that had brought us there and those that were to follow.

～

It was about halfway through our second season when we had stopped kidding ourselves. We wouldn't be going to Australia or Thailand or Florida next year; La Peñita would be our winter home, at least for the foreseeable future. It was no longer the weather or the beach or the prices that was keeping us here. It was the people. It was Roberto and Sergio and Don Pedro, who ran the largest supermercado in town, who always greeted us with a smile and the few words of English that he knew. And it was the Nord Americanos who came back year after year. We had met folks who had been coming for ten of fifteen or even twenty years. And then there were people like Kenny and his wife Laura who had made this their permanent home.

"I'm afraid we'd have to double the rent again," Kenny had told us when we had gone to see him about renting for a third year.

"But I'm not sure if I want to rent them," he added. "I'm thinking of turning the units into condos."

The thought of buying property in any foreign country was enough to send cold shivers down my spine. There was the need to plough through pages of legal documents in what might as well have been Greek, coupled with the fact that the laws and regulations here seem to be 'fluid' at best and legal interpretations seemed often to be open to the highest bidder. And then there was the land registration system which our friends had all told us was as organized as a Chinese laundry. All in all it was a daunting proposition.

So, of course, we said yes. After all, what's life without a few chances? Besides, we certainly didn't want to be priced out of the market.

"If you do go ahead and convert it to condos," I replied, "we'd be interested in buying one."

The lump in my throat betrayed my false bravado like the furtive glances of a young man impressing his friends by lighting up a joint in front of a donut shop full of cops.

And so our journey began. Or should I say journeys.

Our first trip to the office of Lic. Armando Manuel Ortega Gonzalez was in March of our second year. We had gone to sign the Purchase Agreement. The office was in Tepic, a two hour drive up and down the sides of two mountains. And Señor Ortega Gonzalez did not take appointments.

The waiting room was packed when we arrived. Stiff-backed wooden chairs full of locals lined both walls; they were clearly working class folks hoping that the first cousin of the Minister of Finance could help them extricate themselves from whatever criminal or bureaucratic misadventure that they had stumbled into. Young businessmen in well-worn suits were accorded seats on the leatherette couch; they were here I assume to find out how much it would cost to get around whatever bylaws were currently restricting their operations. As the only white folks in the room, the smiling secretary assumed we were the ones with the most cash, so she graciously escorted us to the large table in the centre of the room and whispered a couple of quick words into the ear of Lic. Armando Manuel Ortega Gonzalez.

"Please excuse the mess," he informed Kenny and his wife Laura in perfect English, with a broad smile. "My office across the street is being renovated."

I could guess that was where our legal fees were about to go.

The warm embrace that followed did cause me some trepidation. It was clear that he had done business with Kenny and Laura before.

"The legal system works quite differently here," Kenny had explained on the way up.

"No shit Sherlock," I had thought to myself, although the difference Kenny had gone on to explain was something that I had been unaware of.

We were used to a system where each party in a property transaction has their own legal representative who looks out for their interests. In Mexico, a Notario, such as Lic. Ortega Gonzalez, is responsible for ensuring that the rights of both parties are respected in the transaction. It is a system that makes a lot of sense in a country populated largely by people living on the edge financially, but it gives the Notario lots of power. And much as we trusted Kenny, it was a little unsettling that this would be our one dealing with the Señor, whereas Kenny would be bringing him a whole condo full of prospective clients.

We were certainly not reassured a minute later when the pretty young secretary who had led us to the table arrived with a thick wad of bills which Lic. Ortega Gonzalez stuffed in his jacket pocket without bothering to count.

It was a scene that was repeated often enough that, by the time we were ushered into a small cubicle to actually conduct our business, the gregarious first cousin of the Minister of Finance has wads of cash stuffed in every available pocket. We knew that the restaurants and stores of La Peñita refused plastic and demanded cash, but it was still a surprise to us that legal services also operated on a cash basis.

It was not Lic. Ortega Gonzalez who actually met with us; he was much too busy meeting and greeting and stuffing money into his suit coat. It was his flunky Luis who was assigned to help us finalize the Purchase Agreement. Luis proceeded to take the next two hours explaining why it would take too long to walk us through the one page Spanish agreement in English.

And so we headed back to Canada the next week, having signed an agreement that we only vaguely understood. We had settled on a price and agreed on what renovations needed to be done.

The changes to our own unit were fairly minor. The bathrooms were to be brought into the 21st century and a gate was to be installed and a privacy wall built, to prevent anyone from the street from going up to the roof and walking down the wrought iron stairs and straight into our bedroom. Kenny's tale about the crack heads stealing all of his light bulbs had encouraged us to make that one a 'show stopper'.

The changes to the building itself, which had formerly been the Santa Ana Hotel, were substantial. Along with the rest of the tenants, we spent much of that winter dreaming, usually after consuming one-too-many margaritas, of ways to make condos out of the hodgepodge of single hotel rooms, two bedroom units, up and down one-bedroom units and units that had formerly been up and down two bedroom units, before someone cemented in the staircases. We argued over what to do with the odd patios and decks and the winding wrought iron staircases, that were so narrow that ascending was no problem, but descending after a couple of Coronas and too much dinner was certainly a challenge.

And so we spent the following summer learning all about the intricacies of Mexican real estate. We learned about Hurricane insurance. We read all about the 'ejidos'.

"Ejidos," I explained to Anne, "as far as I can determine are some kind of council of prominent citizens who control some plots of land. They can basically decide who can buy it and who can't. I'm not sure I have it all right."

"Sounds like you know enough to know that it's land to avoid at all costs."

"Looks like it, since pretty well anyone in town could get you evicted from the property you thought you bought, just because they didn't like the look of you."

And we studied up on Bank Trusts. Foreigners cannot own land within fifty kms of the ocean in Mexico; they have to control it through a Bank Trust. While this sounded daunting at first, when we thought about it, few of the people we know are mortgage-free in Canada so it's really not all that different here.

And then there was 'title insurance', a concept quite unfamiliar to Canadians. It is basically a policy that means you get your money back if there is a problem with the title. We had heard all the horror stories. People who had arrived back for the winter to find squatters occupying their homes. A homeowner who had someone show up at their door claiming that their great great grandfather owned this property and had never surrendered title, although they would be willing to 'look the other way' in return for a paper bag filled with US dollars.

Mind you, we had learned over the last couple of years that, like a margarita, you had to take all these stories with a healthy grain of salt. La Peñita is a town where pretty well everyone has lots of time on their hands. But even so, our experiences with Mexican bureaucracy had led us to conclude that the odds of the land registry operating with the efficiency of a Swiss watch were about the same as the odds of us winning the lottery. Twice. So title insurance seemed like a pretty good investment.

By the end of the next summer I had emailed and phoned the people at Stewart Title, or Stuart Little as Kenny liked to call them, enough times that I was half expecting to be on their personal Christmas card lists. There were the regular updates to let them know that "yes, work is moving ahead on getting the condo regime approved and the title finalized."

Then, once it was done, we jointly followed the progress of the documents that Kenny had sent them by overnight courier as it spent two weeks on a burro somewhere as it made its way from La Peñita to Mexico City. There was the flurry of emails as we arranged payment, wiring the money to some numbered bank account in Houston Texas, since a cheque can take up to three months to clear. By the time the leaves had turned colour the next Autumn, Señor Carlos Luis Padilla Reyes from Stewart Title had become simply 'Carlos' and I was just 'Dave'.

Our third winter in La Peñita brought three more trips up the dangerous mountain roads to the office of Lic. Armando Manuel Ortega Gonzalez before the deal was finally closed. Sort of. It was eleven months, three days and twelve hours after that first journey. There was one trip to finalize the Condominium Regime. I quite frankly forget the purpose of the second trip.

"Señor Armando Manuel Ortega Gonzalez will not be in the office today," the smiling and gracious secretary politely informed us, as we watched him sneak out the back door for an early lunch.

And then there was one final trip to sign off all the documents and actually pay up.

Luis had gone back to his regular job in accounting, which may or may not have included collecting and counting all the cash in his boss's pockets. His replacement was Señora Maria Consuela Gonzalez Barrara, the Notario's niece who had either graduated from law school, was going to law school or maybe just knew where the law school was; we were never quite sure. She was certainly more technologically knowledgeable than her uncle so she was able to successfully avoid responding to our emails as well as our phone calls.

But there was one more moment of panic. It happened on our final trip to Tepic. We had gone to lunch that day, Kenny and Laura and Anne and I, to celebrate the conclusion of our business. There was a fifth man who had joined us.

He was a friend of Kenny's, a land developer of some description from La Peñita who wore aviator sun glasses and a Tilley Hat. He had met Kenny at the office of Lic. Armando Manuel Ortega Gonzalez and they had concluded business of some sort as we waited for our turn to come. We had no idea what the nature of their business was, but it seemed to be a particularly thick bundle of bills that passed from him to Kenny to the secretary and then on to the shirt pocket of Lic. Ortega Gonzalez.

There were three messages sitting in the queue when I checked my email that night. There was a note from my bank back in Canada telling me that, as instructed, they had deposited the money for the condo purchase into an account at a Lloyds Bank somewhere in California. It was a transaction that would no doubt raise flags at Revenue Canada and the Royal Canadian Mounted Police. There was a note announcing a special edition of the Jaltemba Sol, our local on-line newspaper. The headline screamed: 'Local Land Developer Arrested for Fraud.' And beneath the headline was a picture of our lunch companion in his trademark aviator sun glasses and a Tilley Hat. The arrest had been made that afternoon on the highway from Tepic to La Peñita. And lastly, there was an email from Kenny:

> "If you've seen the Jaltemba Sol, don't worry. The business I did with him had nothing to do with the condo."

We certainly did worry, but our trust in Kenny and Lic. Ortega Gonzalez proved to be well placed.

But there was one last step before everything was legal: the registration of the title and the condo regime. It is a process that generally takes a couple of hours in Canada.

"In Mexico," Señora Maria Consuela Gonzalez Barrara had explained, "it normally takes six to eight weeks, although we have had some cases where it has taken a couple of years."

I presume that those in the latter category were people who chose an overnight courier service to get the documents delivered.

It was three months later when Kenny called to tell us that Señora Maria Consuela Gonzalez Barrara had told him that "there could be some delay because the staff who do the registrations were engaged in a 'work slowdown' as a result of a labour dispute."

We did have to wonder how anyone noticed.

It would be another six months before we got the call from Kenny to tell us that everything was finally registered and legal. It was mid-October and seventeen months after our first journey to the office of Lic. Armando Manuel Ortega Gonzalez. I was sure that, with our help, the renovations to his new office were now complete.

"Shall I send it by overnight courier," Kenny had asked with a laugh. "Or should I just hold it until you get here."

We chose the safe course. After all, we would be heading south in another two weeks and we wouldn't want the courier to get here after we'd left.

The Overnight Courier Awaits

13.
JESUS, MR. ED AND THE VIRGIN MARY

We must be in heaven – Jesus delivers our mail.

It was one of the perks of being a homeowner that we discovered during our third winter in La Peñita; we got our mail delivered right to the door. And unlike Canada Post, when we headed north for the summer, we didn't even have to pay someone to not deliver it.

There is an old movie entitled 'The Postman Always Rings Twice'. Well, here in La Peñita, he just blows his whistle once. His name, we found out, was Jesus and he rode the streets of town on an old bicycle, whistling at the doors of everyone who is due to get a letter. It can not be an easy job: few of the streets have names or numbers posted so he has to guess who's who. Until we put a sign in our window, all our mail went to the lady next door; and then once we put one up, we started getting the mail for the whole building.

Anxious to see how efficient the system was, and being too impatient to wait the six or so weeks for a letter to arrive from the frozen north, we sat right down and wrote ourselves a letter. It drew some puzzled looks from our old friend Sergio, the postmaster in Guayabitos, when he handed it to him but it arrived in two days. Now, if they could only get the overnight courier service to work that fast

Getting internet in the apartment was another big advantage of home ownership. At first we had hoped to just tap into the connection of our former landlord Kenny, who had moved into the unit at the far end of the building, and we had even brought a router from Canada. Unfortunately, like a lot of other things here, it operated at too high a speed to work properly in Mexico. Kenny's signal extended only as far as his doorstep and since it was too bright to see the screen during the day, I had to wander over there at night with my laptop to do my email. It was after Kenny's wife Laura's second heart attack, as she stepped out into the night and walked right into some strange man typing on her steps, that I decided to explore getting our own connection.

Getting internet without having a phone was certainly no easy task, until we were referred to a young man named Joel who taught computers at the local trade school. I'm not sure what the do-hickey he installed was called or how secure it was, and you had to make sure the little plastic antenna was aimed correctly and hold your mouth a certain way, but it worked. We had high speed internet. I could compose 'Our Mexican Journal' with no fear that all the r's would disappear. I no longer had to guess what 'cut' and 'paste' were in Spanish or what strange combination of keys was necessary to enter an '@' sign. And when we found out about 'Skype', a voice over internet program, phone cards became a relic of the past. It was cheaper to call Toronto from La Peñita than it was from within Canada. It was a whole new world.

"Where do I pay the monthly fee?"

"I come here," Joel replied, eyes wide.

And sure enough, on the first of every month, like clockwork, he would drive up in his beat up old green Chevy and collect the 400 pesos, or $40, for another month of service. For all I knew,

I was somehow secretly tapping into the Mexican army's secure computer network but I really could care less. It worked.

But if it was having the internet that made my day, Anne's was equally pleased with having laundry facilities in the building, thus eliminating the need to haul all our laundry down to the lavanderia. At least most of the time. The popular brand of appliances down here is Mabe, as in maybe it will work and maybe it won't. And there was one day where it quit, just before the spin cycle. And so, off we went, a load of wet but clean clothes in hand.

She was a pleasantly plump middle-aged Mexican housewife, eager to help out the poor gringos who were clearly unaccustomed to manual labour. She smiled as we loaded the clothes into the washer. She pointed politely to the lady at the table in the back with a ledger sheet and a watch as we searched in vain for a coin slot on the machine. But she gave up on us shortly thereafter when she offered us soap and we replied "no necesitamos gracias; *we don't need any, thank you*."

I'm not sure what she was muttering to herself as she walked away but I was sure I heard the Spanish equivalents of 'maid' and 'vacation' in there somewhere.

Owning changed our priorities that third winter. We were into decorating now. Kenny had done a great job with the renovations but there were those little touches that we wanted to add for ourselves. Anne did some nice stencils on the outside walls. We put up light fixtures to replace the bare bulbs which are pretty standard fare in these parts. And we painted the floor of the balcony a vibrant orange; it had been red with splotches of white where the workers had painted all the trim without the benefit of a drop cloth.

"No es semi gloss," I had patiently explaining to the young man at the Comex store when we returned with the paint that we purchased that had turned out to be flat.

His puzzled look had told me that the flat motion I was making with my palm was clearly not translating.

"Necesito semi gloss," I had repeated. I had discovered that, on many occasions, if you repeated the same phrase a few times with slightly different inflections, a light would sometimes go on.

"Ah," he had said in that aha moment, "semi gloss."

And then he had taken out a bottle of some magic elixir that turned out to be 'gloss', poured some into our can of paint and stirred. And presto chango, we had semi gloss paint.

But there was one construction fault that we never could quite solve. We had some sort of odd virus growing in one of the walls. We cleaned it with acid. We re-plastered. We painted. Nothing seemed to fix it.

"Our best hope now," I finally said to Anne "is that it will take the shape of something useful like the Virgin Mary so we can make some money off it."

She furrowed her brow.

"I saw it on TV. There's a restaurant in Colexico, Mexico called Las Palmas. They had an image of the Virgin Mary appear on one of their food grills. People have been flocking to see it."

She stood silent.

"And there was a window with the image in Jesup, Georgia. And weirdest of all, some family in Bryant, Texas claims that they had the image appear in bird droppings on the side view mirror of their pick-up truck. Honest, I think I'm on the something. Move the painting over a little to cover the left side of it."

Anne ignored me as she completed the final decorating touch. She hung the gift that our maid Ramona had given us in Chapala – the picture that her husband had done in prison - in a place of honour: It was the one decoration we had so far that really did tell a story.

There was paperwork to do and bills to pay. A property tax bill of $39 a year, including a $5 fine for being a year late, went a long way towards explaining the condition of the roads, and the fact that we had to pay forty cents a week to get the garbage collected. And we were both pleased and disappointed when the first hydro bill arrived in our name. Pleased because we filled out the Spanish contract correctly and the next bill came in our name. Disappointed because we filled out the contract correctly and the bill didn't go to someone other than us.

You can equip and maintain a place in La Peñita without ever leaving your house. Everything is available door to door here. There are the services you expect: Ciel delivers drinking water by the jug and a tanker truck delivers tanker loads of water for other purposes. There's a propane truck that roams the streets playing an annoying little ditty that must make the driver bonkers by the end of the day. There are a lot of farms in the area so the farmers come into town with pick-ups chock to the gills with pineapple or watermelons or jicama. And then there are others loaded down with baked goods and cleaning supplies and mattresses and shrimp. Not all in the same tuck of course, although even that would not have surprised us.

But the vendors also come on foot. They wheel around trolleys loaded down with pillows or chairs or wall cabinets. And on Friday nights, there is Mr. Potato Man who wheels a wood furnace down the street selling baked sweet potatoes, loaded down with cream. There is a door-to-door sharpening service. The bulk of his business is machetes, since pretty well everyone here has one or two; they are the Mexican equivalent of a weed wacker. We wanted a photo one day but the only thing we had that remotely needed sharpening was a paring knife. I'm sure the guy put his back out doing it.

But there are, of course, other people wandering the streets for a quite different purpose.

"You have to be careful," Bob noted one day as we chatted over drinks at Mateja's Bar and Grill. "There are all kinds of scams out there."

We had heard all kinds of stories in the past but most of them started out with "I heard about someone who" or "a friend of a friend of mine." So we took them all at less than face value. But, as new homeowners, we wanted to know what to look out for and Bob and Joan were neighbours who had been coming to the area for a number of years. When they began their yarn with 'we' instead 'someone', our ears perked up. It was good to hear a tale which, it turned out, came straight from the horse's mouth.

"We were in the yard last year," Joan began, "when an elderly man came knocking on the door. He had a hang-dog look and one of those big old-fashioned sombreros."

"The kind every first time tourist down here brings home?" I asked.

"Exactly," Bob replied. "And then tries to cram into the overhead bin."

"What caught us by surprise was his perfect English," Joan continued.

"I own the lot next to your hacienda," he had told them. "My horse was grazing there and he touched your electrical fence."

"He choked back tears," Bob said, "as he pointed to our warning sign and told us how the poor horse had been electrocuted and died on the spot."

"You must pay compensation," he had told them.

"There was only one problem with his story," Joan continued. "Our last caretaker was an electrician by trade and when he couldn't pay his electricity, he rewired the whole property so that everything was hooked up to our meter. When we got it redone, we didn't bother to electrify the fence. We figured the sign would be enough of a deterrent."

"I told him there was no electricity in the fence," Bob added. "He didn't skip a beat."

"Yes I know," he replied, "but my horse saw the sign and he died of shock."

A horse that could read. That was even better than that old TV hero, who's theme song we sang all the way home that night:

"A horse is a horse, of course, of course.
And no-one can talk to a horse, of course.
That is, of course, unless the horse, is the famous Mr. Ed."

14.
CURVA PELIGROSA

Chuy sat at the wheel of his rusted-out 1983 black Ford Pick-up with the four bald tires and the cracked back window. Relaxed. Comfortable. Confident.

I, on the other hand, had my fingers dug up to the knuckles in the rips and tears of the leatherette of the passenger seat - the scars undoubtedly having been made by the many others who had had the pleasure of traveling with him.

Mexicans normally drive on the right side of the road, but here we were on the left. Chuy had pulled out almost precisely at the road sign showing two cars side by side in a red circle with a bold red line through the middle, a sign whose message I must have obviously misinterpreted. The semi hauling two trailer loads of Corona Beer to thirsty patrons in Puerto Vallarta belched black smoke as it inched its way up the side of the mountain. It was clearly moving much too slowly for Chuy.

Mexicans are, by nature, a very patient people. I have seen them line up for hours without complaint at the Bancomer Bank just to do fifteen minutes of business. I have seen them sit stoically on the sidewalk in the hot afternoon sun still waiting for their buddy who was supposed to pick them up at ten that morning. But something overcomes them when they get behind the wheel and they have no compunction to risk life and limb to save two minutes off the hour long drive from La Peñita to Puerto Vallarta.

It is my theory that Mexican men have spent their whole life taking orders — from their bosses, from the gringos, from the politicians and policias and even from their señoras. But here on the road, they are the equal of anyone. They are finally in control of their own fate.

Unfortunately, Chuy was also in control of mine.

"I learn English in Cincinnati," he announced proudly.

"Really"

"Construction — condominio"

"Oh"

"In 1976 — work with my brothers"

I kept to single word answers, hoping to convince him to turn away from me and focus on the sight that my eyes were fixed upon: the line of cars hurtling down the highway towards us.

"No problema," Chuy said with a sly wink as he slid back into the right lane a few inches in front of the lumbering Corona truck. A man in control.

As we reached the summit and began the sharp drop down into the next valley, I couldn't help thinking about how driving in Mexico had been such a barrier to my attempts to learn the Spanish language. It took me many trips to realize that "Curva peligrosa" didn't mean "Good Place to Pass", but instead meant "Dangerous Curve." Spanish is a language that, like the people who speak it, never seems to be in any hurry and often takes twenty words to say what fifteen will do in English. So it was a mystery to me that the three simple words "Obedezca las señales" could mean "Obey the Signals – But Only If You Really Feel Like It."

I had known Chuy for a couple of months now. He was doing some renovations to the apartment next to us. I watched him carefully and painstakingly plaster and paint the walls. I had watched him lay the tile floor. He was on the far side of sixty, with a thick patch of grey hair and a weather-beaten face that told of many hours of working outside in the hot summer sun.

"Non, non, vamos," he implored me when he had found out that morning that I was going to take the bus to the Home Depot in Puerto Vallarta. He smiled broadly as he pointed proudly to the beat-up Ford.

I was in search of a new bathroom vanity. I knew it would be tough to haul back on the bus and, even if they would deliver it, with just one item, the odds were that we would be back in Canada long before it arrived.

I nodded towards the apartment where he was working. It was mid-January and I knew full well that Chuy had promised to have had the work completed two weeks ago.

"Mañana," he replied dismissively. Mañana, I had learned, is a multi-purpose word in Spanish. Sometimes it means 'morning'. Sometimes it means 'tomorrow'. But most of the time it means 'whenever'.

I knew that my neighbours were not due in town for a couple more weeks so I figured another day wouldn't hurt. I shook my head yes and fished some money out of my pocket to help pay for the gas.

"Non," Chuy replied forcefully, signaling his displeasure that I had even offered. "Cervezca," he offered a moment later as a compromise. His broad smile told me that, by the time all was said and done, this trip was going to cost me a lot more than the bus.

It was almost ten when we pulled into the parking lot at the Home Depot. I handed thirty pesos to the young man in the parking lot to wash Chuy's truck while we were in the store. I figured it was the least I could do.

"Stupid gringo," I imagined Chuy muttering to himself as he rolled his eyes. "It will be just as dirty by the time we get home."

The arrival of Home Depot in Puerto Vallarta was a momentous occasions for the North Americans who inhabit this part of the coast. We all hoped that we would be able to find everything we wanted under one roof rather than to have to shop at half a dozen smaller stores. And maybe some day we will.

I remember our first trip to Home Depot. We had found the grand prize: a propane BBQ. While that might not sound like a huge coup, it was a rare find indeed by Mexican standards. We had spent two years cooking on lump charcoal on a little disposable BBQ. Lump charcoal is an interesting material that you have to light with lighter fluid, something which goes by the safe sounding name of Quick Start in Mexico, doing your best to avoid leaving a line of flame running across the balcony. It generally takes an hour or so to heat up and is pretty much guaranteed to reach the perfect grilling temperature about ten minutes after you have finished eating dessert.

Since the BBQ was clearly too big to haul back on the bus, we agreed to have it delivered. We left the store nervously clutching a form of some sort, the contents of which were a mystery to me. We were only marginally comforted by the smiling salesman's assurance that our BBQ would arrive in La Peñita "mañana". It turned out that he intended the third definition of the word: whenever.

Mañana came and went, which was more than I can say for our BBQ.

It was with some trepidation that I headed down to the main Avenida the next morning, phone card in hand. In the days before we discovered the convenience of phoning via the internet, a phone card was our only means of calling the outside world. There are payphones that accept these cards located throughout the town and, on occasion, some of them actually work. MexTel has taken care to place them as close to the road as possible on as many busy streets as they can so that any attempt at conversation is easily drowned out by a passing garbage truck or the shouts of a vendor hawking watermelons from the back of his pick-up. It really is an excellent marketing strategy; it's a rare time indeed when one is able to complete a full conversation on a single phone card. It's no wonder that Carlos Slim, the owner of MexTel, rivals Bill Gates as the richest man in the world.

My first phone card allowed me to navigate my way through enough of Home Depot's Spanish automated voice response system to reach the right department. With the codes memorized and my fingers working as quickly as possible, the second card allowed me to reach a live person. Unfortunately, by the time he was able to find someone who was able to "habla ingles", the irritating beep told me that I only had enough time left to yell "name" and "call right back" into the receiver. Success came on the third phone card – if you can call it that. At least now I had a name and number and another promise that the BBQ would arrive "mañana".

It was late the next day when Anne and I heard the excited shouts of our neighbours Pat and Bruce just as we were about to fire up the little disposable BBQ.

"Your BBQ's here! Your BBQ's here!"

It turns out Pat and Bruce, having heard our tale of woe, had been biking back from downtown when they spotted a Home Depot truck, a BBQ in the back, driving aimlessly around the streets of La Peñita. Like a police escort, they had led the poor souls to our place on their bikes.

∾

At least today, thanks to Chuy, the delivery of our new bathroom vanity would not be a problem. Although, I wasn't sure which was worse, given the harrowing ride in?

"Lo siento. No tengo," my salesman Juan reported, still smiling, as he trudged back from the stockroom.

Fifteen bathroom vanities hung in the showroom taunting me. We were on try number five, progressively getting further and further from the detailed description that Anne and given me of what she wanted. It was a description which I had passed on to Juan in a combination of English, Spanish, Spanglish and charades. Unfortunately, Anne was thinking of the Home Depots in Canada where there is a much stronger correlation between the models on display and the models which are actually in stock and available for sale.

By the time Juan headed back in search of option number eight, I was beginning to get desperate.

The smile was even broader as he returned with a vanity that matched the original description almost perfectly, but bore no resemblance to any of the models on display. Bingo. Sale.

As I hauled out my treasure out to the truck, I saw Chuy patiently sitting on the sidewalk with his modest purchases. He was saving his impatience for the drive home.

15.
STICKERS AND BONES MAY BREAK MY STONES

"No carro?" Maria asked, shrugging her shoulders.

I stood before her, holding her baby. His body was limp; his eyes flickered open and closed. He weighed somewhere in the neighbourhood of fifty pounds and in his semi-conscious state, it was all dead weight.

His name was Canela and a muzzle was tightly clamped around his jaw.

Although I hadn't yet come across the phrase 'Él muerde' in Spanish class, when Maria clamped her teeth together twice in response to my quizzical look, it's translation became crystal clear.

When we had first come to the area, there were dozens of starving dogs on the street. There was 'Brian', who we named after Brian Wilson of the Beach Boys, since we originally found him on the beach in the next town. A couple of days later we were on the beach here and he came wandering along looking for us. Sometimes if we nodded off on the beach or got lost in a book, we'd wake up and find him sleeping next to us. He would hang out for a while, follow us back to the apartment for dinner, admire the empty double bed and then head off again.

There was 'Internet', who slept on the Internet Café stairs and 'Sandy', who slept on a huge pile of sand near the bridge to La

Peñita. 'Taco's' owner had the taco stand on the corner that got its electricity through an extension cord that ran right across the main street. We named 'Scarface' after the war wound that marked his snout; like clockwork, he arrived every morning for breakfast. And then there was 'Psycho'. Psycho was a little whack-job who lived around the corner from us. He liked to hide in the bushes and jump out at you when you walked by at night.

But Jaltemba Bay Animal Rescue does wonderful work. By our third year in Jaltemba bay, there are a lot fewer street dogs, although the problem was certainly far from solved.

As Mexican landowners, we had decided that it was time to give something back to the community that had welcomed us. Besides, you can only put in so many days at the beach or on the golf course.

And so, when the call had come out for volunteers to help the group out at their monthly spay and neuter clinic, we were quick to sign up.

There were lots of retired nurses and doctors and dental hygienists to help out with the more technical work like assisting in the operating room or preparing the dogs and cats for surgery. And so Anne and I were assigned the traditional newbie jobs: cleaning the kennels and helping out in recovery.

I had been in recovery, the spay and neuter kind not the AA kind, for about three hours when the call came. I was confident that I had mastered the skills required to work there: the ability to detect a heartbeat in a comatose Chihuahua with an old second hand stethoscope, the patience to count out breaths and make sure they fell within the safe limits posted in a chart on the wall, and the fortitude to surprise an unsuspecting patient by ramming an ice-cold thermometer up their butt every fifteen minutes. So when Lorraine, who ran the registration desk with the efficiency of a German engineer, asked me to help Maria get her dog home, I leapt at the chance.

I wasn't quite sure why Lorraine had chosen me. I hoped it was because I was the only male volunteer there at the time and not because of my lack of dexterity with a rectal thermometer. But, in any event, here I stood, a block from the clinic lugging Canela in both my arms, with a confused Maria standing in front of me.

Like every dog here, Canela was not Westminster Dog Show eligible. She was part Rottweiler, part German Shepherd and part Great Dane, with, judging from her weight, a touch of Beluga Whale thrown in there for good measure.

Maria spoke not a word of English and it was at that moment that I realized that Lorraine's Spanish was not as precise as she thought. Maria was looking for someone who had a car to help her get home with her precious Canela. She didn't live around the corner. She didn't even live on this side of the estuary that runs through the centre of town. She lived ten blocks away in downtown La Peñita; in the opposite direction from which we were heading. At least she had recognized the mix-up before we had walked all the way up the mountain to Compostelo.

I suppose I could have returned to the clinic, retrieved my rectal thermometer and asked Lorraine to find another volunteer but both Maria and the slumbering Canela had that hang dog sympathetic look that the street dogs here had all perfected. Besides it would be time away from the sickening smell of disinfectant, and worse.

It took most of an hour to walk the ten blocks, with Canela alternately slung over my shoulder like a sack of potatoes or hoisted up on my hip for support or cradled in both arms with his back arched down to within inches of the pavement. I set him down once to see if he could walk on his own and he slowly waddled a few steps on wobbly legs before lying down for a rest. I couldn't help wondering if he was just in on the joke but I scooped him up and carried on anyway. All the while Maria either trundled along beside us or walked impatiently up ahead. Her face was a mixture of guilt and amusement.

I made sure to check his chart when I finally made it back to the clinic. Twenty-five kilos. I could do that calculation in my head: fifty-five pounds. Kilometres and centimetres and grams may still be a bit of mystery to Canadian who grew up with miles and ounces, but, for many of us who spent our teenage years in the sixties, 2.2 pounds in a kilogram is indelibly etched in our memory.

As Anne massaged my aching back that night, I decided that my next feat of volunteering would involve something much less strenuous.

We had met Maryanne and June some time before when we spent a couple of weeks in Los Ayala while Kenny was finishing up our condo. So when they asked one day if I would be interested in helping them teach English at Escuela Primiera Federal Angel Quintero Dominguez, I jumped at the chance. They assured me that no teaching experience was necessary. It was only one hour a week. And, more importantly, they promised me that I wouldn't have to carry any of the kids ten blocks after class.

"We will do the lectures," June told me on my first day of school. "We just need you to help mark their papers and assist them with their pronunciation."

She was from somewhere in East Texas and I had visions of a horde of little Mexican children running around town greeting everyone with a hardy "Howdy y'all."

The school went from grade one to grade six and there were seventy odd students, split into two classrooms.

One held grades one to three; the walls were adorned with faded posters showing the letters of the alphabet and the numbers one through ten. A jug of water sat on a rickety old table in the corner besides a roll of toilet paper, a cheap substitute for Kleenex. The battered student desks bore the initials and romantic fantasies of a hundred previous graduates. The windows to the classroom were barred more to keep intruders out than the keep the students in. After all, when you're eight years old, and the alternative is working a long days selling onyx figures on the beach, learning your 'a,b,c's' isn't a bad choice.

The classroom that held the senior students looked much the same except the posters of letters and numbers were replaced by maps and pictures depicting great moments in Mexican history. And there, in a place of honour at the front of the class was a framed but yellowed photograph of José Santos Godínez, the first elected Governor of the State of Nayarit.

Maryanne taught the senior class and June the junior one. I decided that discretion was the better part of valour and decided to spend my first day with the more senior students, hoping that they would have at least a rudimentary understanding of English.

I quietly sat at the back and listened while Maryanne delivered her lecture. This is a tourist town, so the phrases that she had her ten year old charges repeat were things like "What time can I check in?" and "Does the hotel have a pool?" and "Would you like some more coffee?" Never mind "see Spot run," this was English that would help them find a job.

When she was done, I worked one on one with half the kids while Maryanne worked with the others. They eagerly played the parts of junior waiters and desk clerks. And I reminded them that you had to pronounce the 'h' in 'hello' and that a 'll' in English does not sound like a 'y'.

"This is going to be easier than I thought," I remember saying to myself on the way home.

"Good morning," eight year old Julio said with a sly smile as he politely shook my hand when I arrived for my third week of class. This was clearly a potential future mayor of Los Ayala.

"I'm glad you're here," said June as she handed me a stack of papers. "Maryanne can't make it this morning so I need you to teach the younger kids on your own."

I stood dumbfounded in the middle of the cement courtyard that served as basketball court and soccer field and parade ground and separated the two classrooms from the outbuilding that contained a storage room and a boys and girls restroom. I believe that is still the correct term to use for a facility where the toilets have to be flushed with a bucket of water that you fetch from around the corner.

I looked down at the stack of papers. I had sat in on Maryanne's class the week before so I knew the drill. They were at the letter 'N', so there was a page with six words that started with 'N' – nest and newspaper and nut; number and nurse and nose. There was a sentence with each word for the students to copy three times and a picture of each word for them to colour in. And then there was a page with a find-a-word game; this week's subject was 'fruits'.

By the time I looked up from the pages, June had vanished into the senior class and I knew there was no turning back.

And so there I stood in front of a class of thirty-six eager young students, aged six to nine. Some were eager to learn. Some, just like many of us when we were that age, eager to give the substitute teacher a hard time.

"Nut," I began, pronouncing the word slowly and carefully as I looked for a blank space on the whiteboard to spell it out.

The board was covered with numbers and letters and pictures from students and teachers that had been copied so many times that they had become permanently etched onto the board. The sentence that June had chosen to explain the word was "I eat nuts." But, at this moment, "I must be nuts" seemed somehow more appropriate.

That was the last time that I saw Maryanne that winter. Three weeks was apparently enough to convince her that I wasn't about to run away and since her busy season was approaching at the posada that she managed, I guess she figured that it was time to pass the torch. So June taught the senior students and I took the junior class. And the regular teachers seized upon our English classes as an opportunity to catch a nap in their cars. It was a well deserved nap I found out later, since they both made the white-knuckle commute every day from Los Ayala to Tepic, the place up in the mountains where we had gone to the offices of our Notario: the infamous Lic Armando Manuel Ortega Gonzalez.

I quickly found out that I was learning as much Spanish as my young students were learning English. It did take some time to find six words that started with the letter of the week that would make some sense and be of some use to a six year old Mexican child. "Quiet" proved to be a useful, at least to me, last minute substitute for 'Quaaludes' and I was able to stretch out 'T' for two weeks so that the letter 'X' conveniently fell exactly one week after we had headed back to Canada.

I did have to endure some suspicious parental looks when every child on the streets of Los Ayala greeted me with smiles and waves. But when June announced that she had to go back to the States for a couple of weeks and that I would be completely on my own, I decided to call in the reinforcements.

"Kids like stickers," Anne announced when I asked her to help me out. "Let's get some stickers that we can hand out to the kids when they have finished their papers."

It seemed like a reasonable idea, although I must confess that I was thinking more of some simple gold starts not the fairy princesses and cars that proved to be the only stickers available at the local papaleria. These were stickers with odd shapes and tiny points that has been glued so tight to the backing sheet by the stifling humidity of a Mexican summer that you needed a chisel to pry them off.

The frenzy began about five minutes into class. It was shortly after I had settled into my place at the front of the whiteboard, and seconds after Anne had pulled the two sheets of stickers from her briefcase. I had just scrawled the first of my 'T' words; I believe it was 'toys'. Juanita sat in the front row, in her neat but worn school uniform, carefully spelling out 'T-o-y-s' on her assignment sheet. Her thirty-five colleagues rushed towards Anne in the corner like crazed parents at the Walmart the week before Christmas in search of the last Wii in stock.

By the time the commotion had awaken Raoul, their regular teacher, from his morning nap in the back seat of his Oldsmobile Cutlass, stickers were everywhere. They were on their unfinished papers and on their desks. They adorned every uncovered body part.

Cars it seemed were a recurring theme to my volunteer efforts in Jaltemba Bay that third winter. There was the one I didn't have, but should have, at the Jaltemba Bay Animal Rescue Spay and Neuter Clinic that would have taken Canela, and me, home in comfort. And there was the one I did have, but shouldn't have: the one on the sticker that was now proudly plastered on the forehead of little Julio, the future mayor of the town of Los Ayala.

16.
GENTLEMEN, START YOUR ENGINES

They were beautiful. They were a sign of progress. And they were depressing as hell.

They were baskets that had been made by the Tarahumara Indians from the Copper Canyon. Vibrant reds and greens and yellows and purples with intricate designs, all painstakingly woven by hand.

We had seen those baskets once before. We had watched the old Tarahumara women in their brightly coloured blouses and white hoop skirts, their faces weathered by the sun and wind, weave them on the steps of the Posada Barrancas Mirador.

But that had been eight years earlier, on our dry run for our first winter in Mexico.

∽

I remember reading about the Copper Canyon to Anne from one of our travel guides:

> "The Copper Canyon Railroad runs from Los Mochis on the Pacific Coast to the city of Chihuahua up in the Sierra Madre Mountains, a distance of just under 400 miles. At its highest point it is 8,000 feet above sea level. There are a total of

87 tunnels – in one of which the train actually makes a 180 degree turn inside the mountain – and 36 bridges, the longest of which is over 3,000 feet."

It had been five years since our first trip to 'Why a bee toes' and retirement was still another five long years away when Anne and I had decided that a dry run was in order. We needed to see how we would fare in Mexico for more than two weeks at a time, and in a place where the locals actually outnumbered the gringos. We had four weeks of holidays saved up and the Copper Canyon seemed like a good compromise; it was enough of a tourist attraction that we were unlikely to be the only white faces on the train.

We should have guessed what was coming as we sat in the waiting lounge at the San Antonio, Texas airport, when they didn't announce our flight to Monterrey. The Aero Mexico agent simply walked around the boarding gate area and quietly indicated to anyone who looked like they had a sense of adventure that the flight was about to board.

There were eight people on the flight: a full house. Four sat on either side of a narrow aisle that was so low that I practically had to get down on my knees and crawl my way to Seat 3B.

The good part of being on a small plane was that we were close to the ground and got magnificent views of the countryside. The bad part was that we were close to the ground and got magnificent views of the mountains that seemed to rise far above the plane on either side. We sat wide-eyed as the pilot wound his way through the magnificent Sierra Madre Mountains. It felt like he was playing a game of Flight Simulator at an arcade, except that the price of a wrong move would be a lot more than a few extra tokens.

We had only a short wait in Monterrey before boarding our connection to Puerto Vallarta. We had been close enough to the pilot that we could not only recognize him by sight, but we could even tell what brand of aftershave he was wearing.

"I'm pretty sure that it was him making the coffee in the boarding lounge," I said to Anne. "And I'm almost positive we were late taking off because he had to mop up all the airport washrooms before we could depart."

Discretion being the better part of valour, we spent the first of our four weeks in the luxury of our timeshare at the Sheraton Buganvilias in Puerto Vallarta. There was no sense pushing it; certainly three weeks would be sufficient to test our mettle. But the week passed quickly and it was soon time to head away from the safe confines of Puerto Vallarta.

San Blas sits about two hours north of Puerto Vallarta. It is famous for two things: mosquitoes and jungle boat rides through the Tobora. Having spent summers in the woods of New Brunswick, we figured we could handle the former, and the latter seemed worth a stop.

When it turned out that the young man carrying a gas container down the main street actually spoke English, we jumped at the chance to book him for a morning tour. When he told us to go early, we settled on a 6:00 am start.

We stood shivering in the cold, dark morning the next day. Shivering and cursing. And when 6:30 came and went, we made our own way up to the Tobora and booked another fisherman, who may not have spoken English, but could at least point at the various birds and other wildlife and who, at least, was reliable.

"What time do you have," I asked Anne the next day, as we sat in the tiny little room that served as the bus terminal for the town of San Blas.

"I can't figure it out," Anne replied, "every clock in town seems to be out by an hour."

And as the words tumbled from her lips, two lights went on. San Blas was in Nayarit and Nayarit was in a different time zone from Puerto Vallarta. So while we had cursed our would be host for not showing up, he had undoubtedly turned the air blue with Spanish cuss words when he had showed up at the right time and the gringos had been nowhere to be found.

There were other stops along the route. We stayed at Mazatlan, where we stuck to our plan, and stayed at a little Mexican place downtown, resisting the temptation to stay at one of the grand luxurious resorts at the north end of town. We took an over-night ferry to La Paz, where we had to make a choice between a room with a window and a room with a toilet seat; we chose the later and were pleasantly surprised to find that it also came equipped with the appropriately named 'Bum Brand' toilet paper. And we took a taxi seven kilometres north to a magnificent deserted beach, and then prayed that the driver would actually return at the appointed hour. But Los Mochis and the Copper Canyon beckoned.

Having no idea just how busy the train would be, our original plan was to book our train tickets before we left Puerto Vallarta. But when the operator at the phone number we had found listed as the 'Mexican Railroad Help Line' politely informed us that she didn't have any information on trains, we decided to risk it. After all, this was all about adventure.

We had planned to spend two or three days in Los Mochis before boarding the train when we went into a travel agency, our fingers crossed, to buy our tickets.

"Why on earth would you want to stay here for three days?" she asked, shrugging her shoulders.

We decided to catch the bus to El Fuerte, the second stop on the Copper Canyon Railroad, early the next morning.

"Another margarita," the waiter in the in the black bowtie asked politely that night as we sat at the Posada de Hildago in El Fuerte, waiting for a table for dinner.

Anne and I smiled at each other, content with our choice of restaurants.

"My name is Luis," the young man announced as he walked to the front of the room, "and I will be your guide on the Copper Canyon train."

We must have hit the jackpot.

"For the first leg, you get the best views from the right side of the train but, for most of the trip, you are better to stand on the walkway between the cars."

But all too soon, the waiter emerged to say that the tables were ready for dinner and we got the evil eye from Luis as he realized that we weren't part of his tour group. There are definite advantages to being white in a Mexican tourist area. People make certain assumptions.

It was only moments after we boarded the train at 7:45 sharp the next morning when we learned an important rule of taking a train in Mexico: while you may have reserved Seat 17B, it is quite likely that at least three or four other people have reserved it as well. And even if they haven't, they have no intention of vacating it.

But we planned to follow the advice we had gotten from Luis the previous night, before he figured out who we were or, more precisely, who we weren't. The spectacular scenery was certainly worth the discomfort of hanging on to a small metal railing while the train climbed up, around and through the mountains. At places, the track doubled back on itself and was literally carved right out of the mountains, with a sheer cliff on one side and a steep canyon on the other.

It was around noon, when the train lumbered into our stop for the first night: the town of Bahuichivo. Our hotel for the evening was actually in the next town, so we hopped onto the Hotel Mision 'shuttle' and headed off. Two bumpy kilometres of 'road', and almost an hour later, we arrived in town of Cerocahui, a town, it turned out, with only four hours of electricity a day.

"Tour?" our waiter Humberto asked over lunch.

And so, Anne and I and Dr. Bill, a plastic surgeon from San Francisco who we had met that morning on the narrow walkway between the cars of the Copper Canyon Railroad, hopped in the back of the pick-up truck. And Humberto and Marie, who owned the local Mini Supermercado jumped in the front. And with Marie at the wheel, we headed off the Gallegos Lookout over Urique Canyon.

Unlike similar lookouts in North America, you could certainly get up close and personal at this one. The only concession to safety was a small wooden sign that roughly translated as 'Don't

Fall – Please'. But the view more than made up for the white-knuckle trip there and back, barrelling along a narrow dirt 'road' in a fifteen year old pick-up with bald tires, with about three feet to spare before the ground dropped 6,100 feet straight down into the canyon. In a strange way, the loud squeaks and grunts that the brakes emitted at every sharp bend in the road were comforting, assuring us that there were at least some brake pads left.

Dr Bill's announcement the next morning at breakfast was anything but comforting.

"They tell me there's been a derailment and the train won't be arriving from Los Mochis today," he reported, before adding "but I've arranged with the hotel for someone from the village to drive us to the next town for $100."

The reams of plastic that the hotel staff brought out to cover everything that we owned and had packed in the bed of our driver's pick-up should have been a clue.

"Anything in the back might get a little dusty," Humberto said, smiling.

As I later found out, anything included me. There was only room in the cab for two people besides the driver, and since Dr. Bill was picking up half the tab and Anne was a lady, me and one of the other villagers climbed up into the back and settled in among our plastic-covered luggage.

I'm not sure if road is the correct term to describe the route our driver took as we headed off. Sitting on the side of the truck bed, I was bouncing around like a hunk of styrofoam on the surf. It was not hard to imagine us hitting the next bump and having my wallet launched from my back pocket somewhere out into the Mexican wilderness. I had just casually slipped it from my pocket into my suitcase when the pick-up came to an abrupt stop.

Flat tire. They say that it takes a village to raise a child but in this part of Mexico it took a village to change a tire. It seemed like half the population came out to help our new friend. As a passenger, I'm not in the habit of checking tire conditions before I climb into a vehicle. It sure seemed like a good idea now. The flat tire looked to be in better condition than the other three; they all looked like they were ready to be made into sandal soles. But with the help of the good people of Cerocahui, we were soon on our way.

"Five minutes," the driver said, holding up the fingers and thumb from one hand to make sure we understood, as the truck lurched to a stop and he popped out of the cab,

Since I suspected that the two words represented a substantial portion of his English vocabulary, there appeared to be little benefit to be had in trying to obtain an explanation of what he was up to. And true to his word, he was back in five minutes, empty handed, and off we headed.

It was the same story at the next house. And the house after that. And at every house between there and the Pemex gas station that sat on the outskirts of town. Unfortunately, our driver made the mistake of turning off the ignition, which necessitated half a dozen young, strong men putting their shoulders to the wheel to push the dead truck up to the pump.

"Five minutes", he announced without waiting for us to hop back in, and headed back into town once the truck was functional again. Anne, Doctor Bill and I stood on the side of the road watching the truck rapidly disappear from view, with everything we owned – luggage, wallet, passports, tickets – packed away in the back.

The five minutes turned into ten and then twenty.

And so off I headed into town in search of our belongings. I had barely made it back to the village when along came our new friend, with everything untouched in the back of the truck.

"Spare tire," he said proudly, pointing to the almost new tire plunked in the back.

If we thought the road from the hotel to town was bad, it was a modern super-highway compared to the one to our next destination. A single lane, with two way traffic, it wound its way up and down the mountains. We all held our collective breath at the bottom of each hill as the engine sputtered and gasped and belched black smoke, hoping that it would at least make that one. In places it was not a road at all but merely a dried-up river bed. Along the way, the driver stopped to pick up any and all hitchhikers, including a family of Tarahumara Indians. The ride to Divisidero and the Posada Barrancas Mirador took four hours; it took another half hour to pry my fingers off the truck.

The hotel was perched on the rim of the canyon, with a 6,000 foot drop off our balcony. We looked down at the birds flying in the canyon. By night, the sky was lit with thousands of stars and, off in the distance, you could see dozens of flickering native campfires and hear the far-off clanking of the shackles from their livestock as they wandered through the hills.

But there was one last adventure to be had. Since we had some time before the train arrived the next day, we decided to take a little hike up in the mountains. And since the hotel was unable to find us a guide, we headed off on our own for a self-guided hike to the El Puerto Overlook. On the way down, we were accosted by three locals selling rocks. I'm not quite sure why we would want to buy a rock, but a dollar seemed a modest price to assure our safe passage down the mountain.

It was that morning, new rock in hand, that we had watched them as we waited for our train: the old Tarahumara women in their brightly coloured blouses and white hoop skirts, their faces weathered by the sun and wind, weaving their brightly coloured baskets on the steps of the Posada Barrancas Mirador.

"I guess that's progress," Anne said when we saw those same baskets for the second time.

But this time I hadn't had to ride in the bed of a rusted out Ford pick-up as it huffed and puffed its way through the middle of nowhere in order to see them. We hadn't had to hold our breath as our plane swooped up and down as it picked its way through the Sierra Madre Mountains. We hadn't had to choose between a window and a toilet seat. And we hadn't had to buy a rock.

By our third winter in La Peñita, you could buy the hand-woven baskets made by the Tarahumara Indians from the Copper Canyon in the Walmart in Puerto Vallarta.

"Yeah," I replied disgustedly, "I guess that's progress."

17.
THE YELLOW ROPE

A Break from Diaper Tag

The two old friends sat on the corner, studying all the action on the street.

Four ears perked forward as they watched Francisco navigate the bumpy road on his old rusty bike, an extension ladder hoisted over his right shoulder and a gallon of paint hanging from the handlebar. I saw the one friend stir but a look from his buddy told him that Francisco was okay.

I saw them both lick their lips as they caught the familiar tune from the ice cream cart, charming at first but now just one of those irritating melodies that you can't get out of your head, as the vendor wound his way through the streets to the private school, hoping to beat the parents to the school gate.

And then something caught their attention. A gringa who was still several blocks away. I saw one nod something to his buddy.

I could imagine what the gesture meant: "If she's got a yellow rope with her – run like hell."

And then I saw the two best friends stand up, sniff each others butts one last time and head off their separate ways: Amarillo and Centro.

Amarillo was the new addition to our family. He was mostly yellow lab with probably half a dozen other breeds mixed in there somewhere, with a scar on his ear where he had come too close to a bicycle he was chasing. At least that's what he told us through the animal whisperer we went to see when we had gotten home last year. Mind you, he had also informed us that he was terrified of being kidnapped and used for stud since he was the best looking dog in La Peñita, so we took everything he said with a grain of salt. I guess he didn't realize the significance of his 'operation'.

He had the saddest hang-dog look, something he had clearly worked hard on and which had served him well begging for food during the two years he lived on the street.

The one we simply called Centro certainly looked like a purebred Springer Spaniel. We knew he lived down on the main avenida as we saw him locked up there at Christmas and Easter when the crowds got big and the fireworks got loud. He would drop by most days for a visit. Sometimes he would follow us home as we walked from downtown with our groceries. Sometimes he would catch up with us on our morning walk on the beach.

Amarillo and Centro loved to play on the beach. They raced like maniacs in and out of the surf. They chased the pelicans. They flipped head over heel when they fell in a hole that a local has dug to bury themselves in the sand, a practice that still mystifies me after all this time. They played an energetic game of 'Diaper Tag' – don't ask – with some refuse that they found on the beach that we thought at first was simply a plastic bag.

Centro was one of the few lucky ones. He was well fed and had a loving family. And he had the freedom to spend his day at leisure, running and on beach and exploring the streets of the town. I didn't know if he had yet found out about 'the yellow rope'.

∽

I remember the morning well; it was a year earlier. We were walking home from downtown, loaded with groceries. As we turned the corner they were waiting at our door. I recognized Cynthia, who lived across the street, and the other two women were familiar, although I didn't know their names. And I recognized the little dog – skin and bones, dirty, his eyes glazed over and his legs wobbly – as he stood at their side in the middle of the street at the end of a yellow rope.

We had been feeding him for a couple of months, like many other dogs, and I saw the recognition in his eyes. His tail began to wag as we walked down the street towards him.

They were from Jaltemba Bay Animal Rescue, the folks who ran the spay and neuter clinic, and the little dog was just recovering from surgery.

"We need someone to foster him for a couple of weeks," the pitch began. "We have someone who will fly him back to Vancouver and we hope to find a family up there to adopt him. He's too nice a dog to go back on the street."

I'm sure they knew Anne from her frequent volunteering at the clinic but I had only been there once and they probably didn't recognize me without a fifty pound muzzled dog in my arms.

We knew they did good work and, besides, it was only for two weeks.

Fat chance. I guess I knew deep down that the die was cast the minute we let him into the house, saw that look that he had perfected and let him climb up on the double bed in between us. In truth, it was probably cast much before that.

Maybe it was time the neighbours across the street moved out in the middle of the night and left him behind howling in the street which, unfortunately, is an all too common occurrence in Mexico.

Or perhaps it was the night we went to dinner in Guayabitos with some friends and watched in horror out the back window of the collectivo as he chased us down busy Highway 200, dodging motorcycles and beer trucks and pick-ups, until his little legs gave out. As I look back, when we returned home that night and found him sleeping soundly on the dusty street in front of the apartment, it was probably at that point that he had decided that we were parents that were worth adopting.

We called him Amarillo: Amarillo Casa in full. It means yellow house. We named him after the yellow house where he had lived with what we thought had been his previous owners. It turned out later that they were just like us; they had also succumbed to that look of his and had just been feeding him.

Like most street dogs, he had many names. The locals called him 'Narrone'. Our friends, who claim that he saved them from drowning in the estuary one night called him 'Blanco'. The twins around the corner who had fed him all winter the year before called him 'Buddy'. The folks at the spay and neuter clinic refer to him as 'Caesar'. But Amarillo really didn't care what you called him as long as it wasn't 'Late for Dinner.' It's amazing how a dog who used to go two or three days between meals now grows weak and peckish if his dinner is ten minutes late.

Thirty pounds later, it was time to rebook our flights home. His vaccinations were all in order. A kennel had been purchased. And we had a 'Certificate of Health' from the kindly veterinarian in Bucerias.

"When is your flight? he had asked.

"In two weeks,"

We had watched him scratch his chin and study the calendar.

"Must be within seven days," he had finally said, and then counted back five days from our departure, smiled, and dated the form accordingly.

I know that Air Canada has many good agents but I had had the misfortune to have drawn the agent from hell. But I was calling from Mexico and the temptation to hang up and try again was outweighed by my reluctance to hear "All our agents are busy, please stay on the line to maintain your calling priority" another fifty or so times.

"The weight limit is fifty pounds – dog and kennel," she intoned. "If it weighs one ounce more you will have to leave it in the airport."

I had visions of a pack of overweight terriers foraging their way through Puerto Vallarta Airport looking anxiously for owners who had long since fled the country. Visions of desperate old ladies with a bathroom scale in one hand and a box of Exlax in the other trying to induce Fluffy to poop her way down to the limit before departure time.

"Well maybe he's only forty pounds," I replied, deeply regretting my previous estimate. "I'm just guessing. I haven't actually weighed him."

"So he's lost ten pounds since we've been on the phone?" she replied, much to my amazement.

We decided to fly Delta instead, even though it meant a stopover in Atlanta.

It was a stopover we regretted a week later as we sat on the plane looking anxiously at our watches. We were half an hour late and the connection was extremely tight. I cursed the airline logic that said it made sense to delay this flight to await the arrival of connecting passengers even if it meant that all of us who would be on connecting flights at the other end would be out of luck.

We clutched the little ticket that the stewardess had given us to tell us that 'Fido is on the Plane' and thought of poor Amarillo trembling somewhere down in the noisy bowels of the plane.

I suspect that we arrived in Atlanta, an hour and a half late, at precisely the moment when our connecting flight took off for Toronto. And as we were making our way out through customs and security and then back in through them again, an annoying remnant of 9/11 since we were not even scheduled to leave the airport, I imagined that the last of the stand-by passengers were receiving their boarding passes for the flight on which we had been wait-listed.

Sure enough, by the time we arrived at the gate, our rebooked flight was full. Atlanta Airport is the size of a small city. A half hour later, we had made our way back to the baggage area to claim Amarillo. He was not there

"There is no way that the dog could have mistakenly been put on the flight; it's against FAA Regulations," the harried agent advised us through clenched teeth once we had made our way back to the gate.

"Okay, okay," he reluctantly replied after much pleading.

We watched him mutter away to himself as he strode to check just to satisfy the two raving Canadians. He was drenched when he returned to report that yes, in fact, Amarillo had been put on the plane by mistake but that he had rescued him and we could indeed now retrieve him at baggage.

It was 4:00 am, eight hours later, when they finally found him. In Toronto. In Customs.

"Is he drugged?" the agent in customs asked as Anne and I huddled over the speaker phone at the luggage desk in Atlanta Airport. "He's remarkably calm."

"No," Anne replied, "he's just Mexican."

"Can you take him out for a quick pee?" she added.

"But I need his documentation to let him out of customs."

"I know this was foolish of us," Anne replied, rolling her eyes, "but I guess we were operating under the obviously mistaken impression that we and Amarillo would be arriving in Canada on the same day. His leash and all his papers are still here with us in Atlanta."

There was a long pause on the other end of the line.

"Don't worry. I'll sneak him out. And I'll have someone check on him once in a while. Listen. I know you will be anxious to see him tomorrow but he must stay in his kennel until you leave the terminal."

It was with a mixture of relief and trepidation that we entered the baggage area early the next morning. There he was. In his glory. Spread out on a Delta blanket. He was surrounded by six Delta Stewardesses feeding him Ritz crackers. His skills had not deserted him. The much practiced look was working its charms.

It was cool when we arrived with patches of snow still on the ground. Amarillo stepped out of the car in his new hand-made coat. He had been the subject of many bemused looks and shaking heads as he had stood in the dressmaker's shop in La Peñita being fitted for his new threads. But I am sure he appreciated its warmth now.

It was a whole new world. The 'sand' was white and cold and wet. The 'lizards' were furry and black and climbed trees. The dogs all had owners and stayed in their own yards rather than wandering around town.

He has learned to 'sing' along with Anne's harmonica playing. It was a lesson we have regretted on occasion. Like when we took him to a concert in the park with a band that featured a harmonica player. Or when he suddenly bursts into song in the back seat of the car when a song with a particularly shrill chorus comes on the radio, something we like to call 'carioki'.

And he even provided me with my fifteen minutes of fame that summer, when the Toronto Star published my entry in their best invented words contest:

"Our dog Amarillo loves to ride in the car. If any door is open — front, back, hatch — he's in the car like a shot; he's 'ambidoorstrous'."

But mostly, he just lies in the yard, soaking up the sun even on the hottest July days. Content with his choice of parents. Until, of course, he sees me down at the dock, tying up the canoe with a length of yellow rope. Then, it's under the porch as fast as he can.

And they say dogs don't remember.

18.
HUEVOS MEXICANOS

The Green Subaru Forester was coming up quickly in the rear view mirror. Our friends Terry and Carmen had patiently followed us all the way from the United States-Mexico Border at Laredo. We knew that our insistence on maintaining the speed limit, despite the fact we had not seen one of the distinctive black and white policia pick-up trucks in many hours, was driving Terry to distraction.

As we watched them hurtle down the Sierra Madre Mountains on Mexico 57-D, gaining on us by the second, we knew something was terribly wrong. Car trouble. Bandidos. Corrupt police. All the things we had feared about driving in Mexico ran through our heads.

As they pulled even with us on the four-line highway, Anne rolled down her window to try to get a clue from Carmen as to what was wrong. Carmen waved frantically at the shoulder of the highway. The single word she uttered told us all we needed to know.

"Bathroom"

Terry accelerated and pulled ahead of us and over into the right lane.

We remembered the little hole-in-wall restaurant where we had stopped a few hours before. When half a dozen kids had immediately descended upon our two vehicles looking for a few pesos to wash off the dust, we knew at once that it was not a place that was frequented by many gringos. We watched Terry and Carmen enjoy their Huevos Mexicanos: eggs fried in hot Mexican salsa. Anne and I drank bottled water; we had enjoyed cold cereal for breakfast back in our hotel room in Laredo and fortified ourselves with peanut butter sandwiches along the route.

Terry lurched the car to the right and then back again quickly, deciding that the shoulder was too narrow at that point.

"There is absolutely nothing," I had noted the night before as we had studied the route, "between the border and Matahuela. No towns at all. You might want to have breakfast before we leave."

Another false stop. Probably not enough cover. Another swerve back onto the highway. You could feel the panic, even at a distance of several hundred yards. We backed off, deciding to give Terry lots of time to find a suitable place to stop.

"Ah, no problem," Terry had replied confidently last night. "There is always something." And I guess he had been right. There was something.

It was around the next slow swooping curve in the highway that Terry found the perfect spot. Or maybe it was just that he had become much less selective. By any account, by the time we had pulled in behind him on the shoulder of the interstate, Terry was long gone off into the scrub brush.

Crisis averted, we continued the journey. It was maybe a kilometer down the road and it came into view as soon as we had wound our way around the next bend. The toll booth. The one with the clean, modern restrooms.

We made peanut butter sandwiches for all four of us the next day.

∾

We like to pretend that it was late summer before we decided to drive to Mexico rather than fly for our fourth winter. But, the truth is that the decision was really made on March 27 at 2:00 AM as we sat in Atlanta airport waiting for Delta Airlines to figure out where they had misplaced our dog Amarillo.

We had heard the horror stories but what the heck. You can't believe everything you read. We did, however, decide to stick to the toll roads and avoid a stretch of highway called 'The Devil's Backbone' which our CAA Guide described as "a rocky spine flanked on either side by 1,000 foot drops, where fog is frequent." When our friends Terry and Carmen announced that they had also decided to drive, we leapt at the chance to meet them 'on the streets of Laredo' and caravan through Mexico.

It had been early on the morning of Terry's predicament that we had left the hotel for the Mexican border. Too early. It would probably be intimidating at any hour of the day to have a soldier, young enough to have been working part-time before heading off to high school, rifle through your belonging with the barrel of his AK47. It was doubly so at five in the morning, in the pitch dark.

The air was crisp and you could see his breath but little else. A scarf covered everything but his eyes, concealing his identity from neighbours as well as those passing through the border. His English was limited to nods and grunts.

Friends who had made the journey before had offered all kinds of advice, much of it contradictory. The one common theme was: "get away from the border as quickly as you can."

So when we were sure that our young friend was satisfied and we edged our way out of the search area and saw Terry stopped ahead of us and starting to get out of the car, we simply screamed "Get back in the car" and kept going. It looked like there was only one way out of town and, besides, he would catch up.

I have come to the belief that many of the border rules and regulations in Mexico are made just so that the locals can keep themselves amused. You can bring in food in your car but, if you're hauling a utility trailer, it's illegal to have food in it. Sometimes your tourist card is good for 180 days, sometimes 90, sometimes 60. I think it depends on the day of the week. And then there is the infamous 'Car Permit' that you require to drive your car into Mexico.

"You get it at the checkpoint, about 15 kms from the border," we were assured by friends who had made the journey many times before. And so we drove up to the checkpoint, documents in hand. Confident. Turns out that's just how they do it in Nogales; Laredo is different.

I'm sure I heard the Immigration agent chuckle and add another tally to his sheet as he sent us back to the border. Got another one.

We knew this was not going to be easy when, after stopping twice to ask directions, it took us fifteen minutes to find a parking spot at the Immigration Office. Three line-ups, several pesos and three hours later, we pulled back into the check-point – proper documents in hand. It was four hours and just 15 kms from where we had set out that morning.

The border may have been a nightmare but the drive was a dream. Good road. No traffic. And a ribbon of asphalt that soared and dipped as we made our way up and then down the mountains. Past desert and stands of scrub trees and a hundred variety of cacti. Past dried-up riverbeds. A dozen vistas called out for us to stop and take pictures: spectacular views of picturesque villages nested up in the mountains.

There are two highways between most major cities in Mexico. A toll road, the cuota, the preserve of gringos and the growing Mexican upper and middle class and the libre, the free road, the chosen route of everyone else. The libre winds its way through towns and villages of all sizes and descriptions, each of them marked by a 'tope' or, more often a series of 'topes.' Speed bumps. Some of them home-made. All of them high enough to knock the track off a panzer tank or bring an eighteen wheeler to a screeching halt. The cuota, on the other hand, bypasses every village and hamlet and runs as straight as the topography will allow. The scenery is punctuated only by the sporadic appearance of a giant wooden cut-out of a bull, the significance of which we have yet to determine, and the very occasional outpost comprised of a Pemex gas station and a hole-in-the-wall restaurant where they serve Huevos Mexicanos.

The first tinges of red were beginning to appear in the sky that hung above the great plain that surrounds the city of Matehuela, Mexico. Relief set in as the first traces of civilization came into view and we knew that we had found our first night's destination before nightfall. We had been warned not to drive in Mexico after sunset. It wasn't the bandidos or the sharp turns and quick descents that were said to be the major concern. It was the cows. Up in the mountains, where there is a chill in the air at night, the heat from the asphalt attracts then to the highway. We had seen evidence of the consequences in the ditch a few miles back.

Motel Real Villas sat just where we had been told, on the road into town. Pastel purple walls and soft lights. A tall rounded brick arch entrance, the entranceway graced by towering palm trees.

I leapt from the car and walked up to the darkly-tinted plate glass window that served as a reception desk. I felt a sense of excitement and perhaps even danger, although the odds of running into someone from back home were infinitesimal. There was a slot to slip your money through and a small circle that you spoke into.

I am sure that the receptionist had instruction never to leave the booth when booking in a local. After all, it simply would not do for her to know that the mayor was checking in with someone who was clearly not señora mayor. But I was clearly not a local and it was much too difficult to try to engage in a conversation in pigeon Spanish through the little hole in the glass. After all, how many locals would arrive here with a car full of luggage and a dog? Not many I would hope.

"Diez," she announced, before smiling and adding "Ten" in surprisingly good English. The No Tell Motels that sit on the outskirts of any Mexican city of respectable size, are favourite stops for Nord Americanos, particularly in the Fall and Spring, as they head to or from their winter homes further south. Each room has an attached garage that can be locked for the night so there is no need to pack and unpack all your belongings.

I handed her the four hundred pesos nightly rate – about forty dollars.

"Two hundred for four hours," she had explained, smiling smugly.

I waited for the key but as she spun around and went back into the booth it was clear that we were not about to get one. Once you were here, you were here in for the night.

We pulled into the garage, closed the door and entered the room with no idea what to expect. It was a pleasant surprise. Spotless. Bright. Very well appointed. The Kleenex dispensers on either side of the bed were a nice touch. It was a step up from one side of the room to the other.

"People are different heights," Anne clarified.

It had been a long day and, given the lack of a key, room service seemed like the best option. Besides, in addition to hamburgers and pizza and other staples of a room service menu, you could order rum, tequila, beer and a variety of other libations. Or perfumes, oils, lubricants. Or, for 180 pesos, viagra. I guess that even Matehuela's macho mayor needs some pharmaceutical assistance for an evening with his 'personal assistant'.

We settled for hamburgers and Coronas.

It was fifteen minutes later when we heard the tapping on the large stainless steel canister on the courtyard-side wall of the room. The low scraping sound of metal on metal told us something was spinning inside it. It opened and there on a tray sat two hamburgers, two Corona and a bill. We slipped our money onto the tray and spun it back out into the darkness. Food delivered. Bill paid. Anonymous.

There was even TV in the room. Three channels. None of them were in English but with the dialogue limited to grunts and groans and "Yessss Yessss", it wasn't hard to follow the action. And there was lots of action, both on and off the screen. The garage doors were up and down all night. As I'm sure, were most of the guests.

We left at daybreak, leaving just enough time for the cattle to wander back to their pastures. The drive could probably be done in two days but with six months of dust to be swept up back at our apartment in La Peñita, we splurged and did it in three so we could get there early in the day.

I'm sure there are No Tell Motels in Guadalajara but we had booked a place beforehand. How I craved for the luxury of one as we hauled suitcase and boxes and coolers up four flights of stairs.

We live in a small town in Canada. Rush hour consists of three cars and a school bus. When we go to Toronto, we time our travels precisely so as to avoid the traffic. So I am not sure what possessed us to leave the next day precisely at the height of traffic in a city of seven million where we understood neither the language nor the directional signs nor the rules of the road. Maybe it was the fact that we foolishly assumed that a highway named 15-D would actually be a 'highway' and not the main street of Guadalajara. Or maybe it was just that adventure gene kicking in again.

A left turn is always a challenge here. Sometimes you turn from the left lane. Unless there's a lateral, in which case you turn from the right. Or the left right if it's a two-lane lateral. Or unless it's the weekend, when you are not permitted to turn left at all, or a day with a 'T' in it when you have to turn left even if your destination is to the right. But we had a plan: just follow the lead of a local; they will understand the rules.

The flaw in our plan became apparent at the first traffic light. The one at the busiest intersection in Tonala: a major suburb. The one where traffic was backed up many blocks in all directions. Unfortunately, our plan assumed that locals both knew, and followed, the rules.

When the two cars ahead of us swung into the left lane to turn left, we merrily followed behind them. It was only when the light turned red and a cacophony of blaring horns screeched their displeasure at the dumb gringos, did we realize that our guides had merely pulled over to that side because they knew they could beat the yellow signal. We, unfortunately, could not.

It was probably no more than half an hour, but it seemed like half a day before we emerged from the bumper to bumper mass of traffic on the far side of Guadalajara. We had lost our traveling companions somewhere in the maze. It took several honks to realize that Terry and Carmen's green Forester was two cars up ahead, having somehow passed us along the way.

We lost them again somewhere between Compostelo and La Peñita. It was some time after we had pulled off the toll highway onto Mexico 200: a narrow, winding two-lane road that weaves its way through the mountains to the coast. The views are breathtaking and a marvel to behold, particularly if you are sitting on a bus rather than behind the wheel. The traffic was light so we forged ahead, taking full advantage of the golden opportunity that fate had awarded us.

We figured that Terry could find his way from there. With nothing but cliffs on either side, it's pretty hard to make a wrong turn. But we did wonder if he was sitting in front of the apartment, waiting patiently for us, or back in the brush, recovering from another encounter with Huevos Mexicanos.

19.
PEROGIES IN MEXICO

Traditional Dining Options

When we arrived in La Peñita de Jaltemba for our fourth winter, there were plenty of signs that the town had passed the tipping point in terms of its transformation from a farming and fishing village to a tourist destination. But there were three that really stood out: real estate agents, tours, and food.

There was only one Nord Americano real estate agent during our first year here. He had a small office out on the highway and a good reputation among the Nord Americanos. There were other local agents of course but, from everything we heard, some of them specialized in selling property that they didn't own.

But by year four, there were half a dozen agents who catered to the gringos. They set up booths at the market to flog lots and condos and haciendas. The one condominium development in La Peñita had been joined by half a dozen others and our first timeshare was surely not far behind. And real estate prices reflected the surge in demand.

༄

There were always tours in La Peñita; they were just a little more basic. In Puerto Vallarta, they tour you around in an air-conditioned bus. In the ritzy resort of Nuevo Vallarta, you travel in a luxurious, modern amphibious vehicle. In La Peñita, you sit on a beat up old couch in the back of a pick-up truck.

There were the self-guided tours arranged by one of the social butterflies in Jaltemba Bay. The process was simple. A note was posted for everyone to meet at a local bar, the people with vehicles were paired up with those without, and a caravan headed out to the destinations of the week.

We took one to the stunning El Coral waterfall up in the mountains. There were no signs; the longer term residents knew the way. It was a fifteen minute hike down a narrow and slippery path to the foot of the canyon. There were no guardrails and a steep penalty for any misstep. We dove from the cliffs into the cool, clear pool at the bottom of the falls. And no-one asked for a tip.

We sat on the rocks and drank beer, cooled the natural way, and ate 'Mexican picnic': a chicken salad in a can that you spread on tortillas. Only the far off call of a Macaw broke the silence. Well, that and the cries for help from one eighty year old woman who made it down but couldn't make it back up. Sometimes there is value in a tour guide.

There were the tours that came complete with a guide; a guide being anyone possessing basic English, directions to the local sites and a pick-up – extended cab optional.

We took one to a natural hot springs. There are no cemented-in pools, but the locals had shifted the rocks around to form one large enough area to lie down in. The water got hotter the further upstream we went; we boiled eggs in the stream and the stench of sulphur clogged our nostrils. Roberto, the farmer whose land bore the springs, proudly showed us his property. He scooped out some freshwater shrimp from a cold stream on one side of his meadow and boiled them for us in the hot spring on the other. Our taste buds exploded in ecstasy. We took a wonderful photo of horses shrouded in the steam.

There were stops along the way. Our guide showed us a brick factory, where they make bricks out of cow manure. I guess in Mexico you refer to someone as being 'built like a shit brick house.'

And we stopped at a small country schoolhouse to deliver pencils and treats for the kids. The smiling faces were ample reward. The students were lining their writing paper by hand. There were six in all, eager to learn: three grade ones, two grade fives and one girl waiting to go to high school. The town had had one boy who had made it that far, and was doing well, until he had to quit when his father called him home to help tend the fields. The teacher was a young woman from the village. She was sixteen at most and was shopping for a husband; the only town in which tradition and circumstances would allow her to look was the next village down the way. She told us that she had two boys to choose from.

And then there were the whale watching tours. You can choose three levels of these tours, depending on the tolerance of your liver.

There was the basic tour, where you cram half a dozen people, plus the captain, and a twelve pack of beer into a small fishing boat. We hung on for dear life as the boat went straight up in the air when the captain put it to full throttle to try to make it through the surf, remembering to look for the life jackets only when we were beyond the point of no return. And we held our breath when he brought the boat back into shore and saw the captain leap out and go completely under his vessel as it got caught in the high waves.

Unfortunately, we didn't see any whales on our tour and had to resort to a contest to see who could come up with the best whale joke. The winner:

> Q: What is the most annoying insect on a whale watching trip?
> A: The no-see-um.

Then there was the enhanced tour, where you cram a dozen or so folks into a slightly larger boat, and the price of the tour includes all the beer and margaritas that you can drink. People tended to start drinking early; after all it is five o'clock somewhere. 'Seasickness' hits half the participants, almost exactly at the moment where the boat was at its farthest point from shore. It is then that any whales became an attraction for the half that had chosen to pace themselves and a nuisance for the others, giving the captain a reason to stay out to sea a little longer.

And then there was the party boat tour, where you load a hundred people on a boat that safely holds fifty and dump the life jackets because they are just taking up space that could be filled by an additional celebrant. We passed on that one. The whales were clearly secondary since the music was loud enough to be heard in Tepic, two hours away. And any whales that did come within sighting distance were clearly either deaf or big fans of the Macarena.

But by year four, the air conditioned tour bus made its first appearance in town, offering multi-day tours to Guanajuato and Mexico City, with stays in four star hotels. A sunset pirate cruise cannot be far behind.

∽

But perhaps the biggest change was the food.

We were used to making regular trips to Puerto Vallarta to pick up the items that we couldn't find in Jaltemba Bay. But with each passing year, the list became shorter and shorter. You could buy goat cheese at Poppins in Guayabuitos. And Cricos had light bread and bagels, although you had to know enough to ask for the bagels, as they kept them in a freezer in the back. We had discovered that there were a few things like that; you just had to know who to ask. And the owner of the Bavarian Gardens German Restaurant, where we had listened to our Uncle Jose Gringo friends tell us how Mexican they were, had opened a deli with European cheeses and cold cuts that were something other than ham.

A new Mega Store had opened in Bucerias, which was only half as far away as Puerto Vallarta, with a lot less traffic. It even had tour guides who helped gringos navigate through the maze of grocery shopping in Mexico. And further south in Puerto Vallarta, Walmart and Home Depot had been joined by Office Depot and Radio Shack and a Mexico City chain called Liverpool, which sold every brand name product you could imagine.

But the solution to our greatest shopping dilemma: finding a red wine that had a label bearing neither 'Product of A Country Where They Speak Spanish' nor a penguin had come from a most unlikely source.

"Do you drink?" Anne's gynaecologist had asked at her annual physical.

"Probably too much," she sheepishly replied, awaiting a lecture.

"And you'll be in Mexico for the winter," he continued, as he scratched out something on his prescription pad.

Anne nodded in the affirmative.

"I serve this at all my dinner parties," he said, as he handed her a piece of paper on which he had scrawled 'L. A. Cetto — Shiraz.' "Everyone loves it. They can't believe it's a Mexican wine."

And so our days of hauling three bottles of wine in a backpack on the bus from Puerto Vallarta were over. We could buy good red wine at Don Pedro's Supermercado five blocks away.

And it wasn't just eating in that had changed; there were new options for eating out as well. La Peñita had always had Soleys: a fine Italian restaurante. But now we also had the Xaltemba Restaurante and Galaria next door, which featured fine dining and art exhibits. It had the Improv and a lecture series and a Sunday Night Cabaret and served turkey on Thanksgiving and Irish Stew on St. Patrick's Day.

And then there was Los Potros. The Perez Brothers were an institution in Jaltemba Bay. They were brothers from Los Ayala who played every Friday night at the Bavarian Gardens. There repertoire consisted of a mixture of rock standards, sung with a Mexican accent, and cumbia dance tunes. The cumbia, which was made popular in the mid-1950s by the Mexican musical group 'Los Cometas', sounds like a mixture of traditional Mexican music and rock and roll, and looks like polka on steroids.

It was in our fourth season that the Perez Brothers decided to strike out on their own and open a restaurant: Los Potros. The music was what one would expect but the menu was anything but. The featured item was baked ham – and perogies.

Can a sushi restaurant be far behind?

20.
FIT FOR A PRINCE

Francisco Padilla stood baking in the late morning sun. Still and erect. The perfect soldier. The dark blue uniform attracted the heat like a magnet; the brass buttons reflected like stars in a dark sky. The blue kepi with the gold brocade perched jauntily on his head brought back memories of Claude Rains in Casablanca. I watched him cast a furtive glance at his best friend Arturo and at Soraida, about to be crowned King and Queen.

I wondered what he was thinking as the crowd grew silent and the coronation ceremony began. I was sure it was not the challenges that he and Arturo were about to face; it was more likely the ice cream that his mother had promised him on the way home.

Francisco was six years old; he was about to become the first prince at the Spring Festival at Kinder Miguel Hildago in La Colonia, which sits on the outskirts of La Peñita.

The Spring Festival is a rite of passage for the children of the area. It follows a month of hotly contested campaigning. Brightly decorated Kleenex boxes in every business in town invite you to support your favourite candidate and the children who receive the most donations are crowned as Kings and Queens and Princes and Princesses.

I was pleased to see that the town had had the decency to reject the candidacy of little Gabriela who's sultry pose on her ballot box was disturbingly provocative for a five year old.

The parents, aunts, uncles, friends and neighbours of every student at the school were jammed into the small school-yard. They stood four deep and craned their necks to watch the ceremonies. Grandmothers were afforded the luxury of white plastic chairs and a front row view. I suspected that you could have fired a cannon down the deserted streets outside the walls of the school without hitting anyone; and, given the Mexican infatuation with noise that they probably would be doing exactly that later in the evening.

The second year class, dressed in bright green frog outfits performed a dance routine as a scratchy CD hissed and skipped its way through La Cucharacha. My pigeon Spanish did not allow me to decipher the significance of the frogs as the School Director leaned over and offered some sort of explanation.

A graduating student shouted her way through an ode to the seventh President of Mexico, blissfully unaware that her microphone was working just fine. Tears flowed.

And then it was time for the first year students. They burst from one of the three classrooms that made up the school in their crisp clean white t-shirts and shorts – well mostly clean. Forming two lines, they gyrated their way through what could only be described as a cross between a dance and a gymnastics routine. They watched each other. They scanned the crowd for familiar faces. And sometimes they even watched the teacher.

The señoras in the crowd beamed and nudged each other as they pointed out a daughter, a nephew, a neighbour. The eyes of the señors were elsewhere.

"You're supposed to be watching the children", Anne reminded me, with a sharp jab in the ribs. I reluctantly drew my eyes away

from the tall and striking Señorita Alexa as she swayed and ges-
tured wildly at her students, trying to bring some order to the
chaos. I saw a wave of eyes being similarly redirected.

The ceremony was over far too soon and a warning from Brian had
convinced us to forgo lunch.

"It's the fat from inside the pig's skin", he had clarified for us.
We were grateful that his grasp of the language was much better
than ours. We had been staring at the concoction in bewilder-
ment: some sort of white substance that looked remarkably like
ice, chopped up in chunks, mixed liberally with salsa which, we
assumed, was designed to either add nutrition or hide the taste or
both. It was all served on an over-sized waffle of some sort.

The Spring Festival is one of the social events of the season and
Anne and I, along with our friend Brian, had been invited as
the guests of honour. It was reward for being the most active
Nord-Americanos on the Los Amigos de La Peñita Education
Committee.

"We were going to sit you in the sun," Zobeida, the head of the
school's parent council, had noted with a smile that would have
been the envy of any Canadian politician. Their request was for
a roof to shelter the play area from the relentless sun. They were
still running second to a request from J. Cruz Batista Primary for
a leveling of their yard so the students didn't have to wade through
a foot of water during the rainy season to get to the outhouse.

We thanked our hosts, promising to at least consider amend-
ing our priority list for funding, and made our way out through
the school gates. Anne clutched our parting gift tightly: flowers
carefully and painstakingly crafted from recycled Coke bottles.

And we watched Francisco, the new first prince up ahead as we made our way home that afternoon. His left hand held onto the blue tunic as he dragged it along the dusty street; dirt from the playground was streaked on his dark blue trousers. His right hand held tightly onto his mother as he dragged her down the street. I guessed that a royal treat awaited.

Los Amigos de La Peñita bills itself as a "community service organization comprised of residents of the local community that exists to serve the people of La Peñita, the surrounding Colonias, and the community at large through it's participation in activities designed to improve the lives of area residents."

I can recite those words in my sleep; I helped to write them and I had inserted them in half a dozen press releases by the end of our fourth winter.

We had gone to a couple of meetings of the group the previous year. We had even attended their big fundraiser, Fiesta La Peñita, which was held at the internationally acclaimed estate of Thomas Bartlett. The estate was only a block from the condo, which we figured certainly couldn't hurt our property value, although Mr. Bartlett was probably heard to mutter "there goes the neighbourhood" when we moved next door.

So when we went to the first Los Amigos meeting of the season that fourth year, and there was a deafening silence when the president asked for nominations for the position of secretary, I decided to let my name stand. The Executive were not so much elected as cajoled.

"At least this job doesn't involve carrying dogs," I whispered to Anne.

"Or handing out stickers," she replied.

Unlike my two previous failed attempts at finding something I could do as a volunteer, this was something I actually had experience at doing. I had thirty years of experience in government, so I knew how to write minutes and draft mission statement and do press releases.

Having worked many years in the area of Intergovernmental Relations, I knew the secret to writing a press release. Stick to the message. And write it a couple of weeks before the event. That way you just have to decide if people 'strongly agreed' or 'generally agreed' or 'agreed to disagree', after the event was concluded. And you can have a press release out in two official languages even before everyone catches a plane out of town.

So when Los Amigos has their first beach clean-up, the release was on the Jaltemba Bay Folk Message Board and in our on-line paper, the Jaltemba Sol, before the sun was down. After all, how long does it take to decide that the 'XX people' who showed up for the event were actually 'More than 150'.

It was a busy year for Los Amigos. Besides our work at the schools, there were the beach clean-ups and the children's park we helped build and our scholarship program.

And then there was our plastics recycling program.

I had seen metal recycling in action here. We watched the owner in the house across the street do it. He just put all his cans in a bag, dropped them in the middle of the road and drove his truck back and forth across them a couple of times. But that was just for small loads. When we were in Puerto Vallarta at the bus terminal one year, someone came in with a garbage bag full and they backed one of the buses over them a couple of times. We weren't sure what the next step up was, but if there's one of those jumbo garbage bags on the tarmac when our plane leaves, I'm asking to be on a different plane.

No wonder the locals just shook their heads when we actually bought a compactor to crush the plastics we were collecting.

And as Los Amigos became more and more known, the local politicos began to take notice. Even the 'Presidente Municpale', or mayor as we would call him, showed up at our new children's park one day. He arrived with a cast of about a dozen flunkies, shaking hands and kissing babies, even the older ones, like politicians anywhere. It was just like my old days in intergovernmental relations, except, in this case, they actually sent in an advance guard of police, armed with automatic weapons, to secure the site and stand guard while he chatted up the locals.

And so my fourth winter became full with meetings: breakfast meetings, dinner meetings, back-to-back meetings. General Meetings, Executive Meetings, the Education Committee, the Recycling Committee, the Fundraising Committee, the Public Relations Committee. And for the first time since I had retired, I had to start a day-timer.

And as we exchanged goodbyes and thank yous with Zobeida at the Spring Festival at Kinder Miguel Hildago that afternoon, I thought to myself how much of an honour it had been to have been invited as a guest to an event that meant so much to the community. And how it made the meetings and minutes and press releases seem all worthwhile.

After all, I was not the only one who's retirement plans had been forever rearranged by Los Amigos. My guess is that our president, had not planned to spend his golden years cooking up deals with the Presidente Municpale and his armed guards. And the guys running the recycling program, had likely envisioned fishing and golf and not building wire baskets and sorting through garbage for plastic bottles. I am pretty sure that Brian had intended to take quiet walks on the beach rather than trying to chair a meeting of the Education Committee in Spanish, while avoiding the young children – the ex-officio members of the committee - crawling under the tables. And even those who still worked found time to help out.

Maybe I could be cajoled into serving one more year.

21.
UPPER CANADIAN MEXICANOS

By our fourth season, 'Ou Mexican Jounal' was getting harder and harder to write. I had pumped out an issue every two weeks that first year, filled with the weird and wonderful things we saw. It was down to one a month by year two. Year three saw four volumes and it dropped to two by the fourth.

Somehow, the different customs and sights didn't seem so unusual any more.

I dedicated one of those two issues to a story about a woman I had seen decorating her balcony. I had watched her using cut-off Coke bottles as paint cans. And then, to make cushions for her lounge chairs, she had cut up an old foam mattress into two wide strips, strapped them to her back and biked to the fabric shop. She took up most of the road when she brought them back, four foot long, strapped sideways on her bike carrier. It was the same lady I had seen hauling an empty propane tank to the gas plant in a plastic milk case bike carrier.

That was no lady; that was my wife Anne.

Sure, there are some things you never get used to.

The attraction of fireworks will remain a mystery: fireworks that don't explode in glorious colour but simply make noise. Lots of noise. I still duck when I see a boy running at full speed through the town plaza carrying some sort of gizmo that's shooting out sparks in all directions. I cringe as I see the sparks igniting trees and tarps and the clothing of onlookers; the locals just clap and cheer and urge him to go faster.

It still takes a couple of tries to take down someone's phone number. We have become accustomed to having people dictate their number in a 123-4567 pattern, so a cadence of 12-3-45-67 or 12-34567 still throws me off.

And getting someone's name requires patience since everyone goes by four names: two first and two last.

But there are so many other things that make perfect sense once you get used to them.

It makes sense to make a left hand turn from the outside right lane. At least it does if you're not the one driving. It keeps the traffic flowing.

And why shouldn't going to a bar be a family event. What's the real harm in having junior see the old man have a good time? And if you're at a bar on the beach, what's the big deal in using the tables as a dance floor. We watched one couple even have their one year old up table dancing. In Canada, you'd end up on the national sex offender registry; in Mexico, they give you a free t-shirt.

And the regime of banking fees is much more logical than ours.

"So in Canada, if you have much money in the bank," our friend Chuy had asked, shaking his head, "you pay nothing?"

"Correcto. As long as you keep a certain balance."

"Es loco. In Mexico you pay nothing unless you deposit more than 25,000 pesos a month."

He smiled broadly.

"Solomente notarios and politicos have that much a deposito."

And we had learned to adapt and adjust.

When the refrigerator repairman told us he would be there at nine am, we knew that as long as we got home before noon, we would still have time for a quick lunch before he arrived.

"It's an old joke," Kenny explained. "Why do Mexicans wear watches? So they will know how late they are."

And we were quite comfortable having our teeth worked on by a dentist whose English vocabulary consisted of two words: 'open' and 'close'. The scars on his fingers told us that he even got those two occasionally mixed up.

"If you feel much pain," the pretty, young and almost bilingual receptionist explained, "wave your right arm."

And we didn't bat an eye when the Chief of Police helped Rosalie pour tequila shots down the throats of anyone willing at the benefit concert. Even if he did know that most of them would be driving home in another hour or so.

So when we spent our first Semana Santa in Mexico, we found it more entertaining than frightening. It's the week that concludes with Easter Sunday and the population of Jaltemba Bay rockets from about 20,000 to 50,000. There are tents about six deep along the shore. The beach features portable beer stores, complete with bands and DJs and loud sound systems and vendors sell everything from snacks to iced cappuccino. Water taxis ferry people back and forth between the towns as there is too much traffic on the roads and the 'Party Boat' looked pretty loaded – in more ways than one. But mostly, it was a family affair. Everyone just looked like they were out to have a good time and weren't looking for any trouble.

And when it came time to pack up and head north, the steps we had been given to 'summerize' the condo, which at first seemed counter-intuitive, made perfect sense. Since the humidity approaches one hundred percent in the summer, you can't seal everything up or you'll get mould and a layer of water on the floor. So you leave all the windows open – there are bars after all – and leave every door and drawer open. Mind you, it does make for a big mess on your return, with an inch and a half of dust and the occasional dead spider covering all and sundry.

Our Mexican beach dog Amarillo took a lot less than the four years it took us to adjust to become a 'Canadiense'. It wasn't that he had a lot of choice. When we first arrived, it was snowing and the temperature dipped below zero. He was certainly quite chatty but, fortunately for him, they didn't teach me a lot of cuss words in Spanish school.

When we hiked the infamous trail to Lo de Marcos, the one that it took us five tries to find, with some friends, the locals were pretty amused that the former beach dog now took a taxi to the beach. But it proved better than our options on the way home.

"Perro?" Anne asked the Pacifico bus driver we had flagged down on the side of the road, pointing to Amarillo.

"Luggage?," he replied, indicating the dark compartment crowded with battered suitcases.

We got a better offer from the collectivo; they let him ride inside with the rest of the passengers.

When we suffered the trauma of our car breaking down on the way home that year, and we were 'forced' to spend three days in the spectacular town that is Guanajuato, we ran out of dog food. And so the poor little beach dog who used to eat out of garbage cans was treated to room service.

"An order of chicken and rice por favour," I asked the waiter, and then watched him roll his eyes as I added, "but we don't need any cutlery."

We had become accustomed to Amarillo drawing odd looks. After all, the Mexicans in the neighbourhood think that we are raising some sort of mutant child. They have all been avoiding us since Anne went shopping at the market for two items: a sweater so he wouldn't get cold on the plane and a stuffed animal toy.

"The sweater has to be large enough to fit a six year old," they had overheard Anne say, "but the stuffed toys had to have no eyes because he'll rip them out."

A taxi to the beach, room service, toys and a sweater: no wonder he had such an easy time adapting.

You can take the dog off the street, but you can't take the street out of the dog. So he still enjoyed a game of diaper tag on the beach with his friend Centro. And, despite his experience with the yellow rope, he still felt 'inclined' to participate when any female in the neighbourhood came into heat; participation that resulted in an STD and a week on antibiotics. And he still liked to stand on the balcony and bark down to his girlfriend as she wandered off in search of somewhere to spend the night. We named her Juliette even if our 'Romeo' didn't have the script quite right.

∽

When Anne and I first left Ontario and moved to New Brunswick, a one year adventure that ending up lasting twenty-five years, we were surprised to hear our friends refer to us as 'Upper Canadians.' It was a term I had not heard since Grade 8 Social Studies. And it was not intended to be a compliment.

There were four provinces when Canada became a country: Nova Scotia, New Brunswick, Lower Canada - which became Quebec - and Upper Canada, which is now Ontario. Upper Canada was the rich and sophisticated one; New Brunswick was poor and, in the eyes of Ontarians, the backward one. But New Brunswickers thought of themselves as simply 'practical'.

"Upper Canadians have more money than brains," our new neighbour explained. "They buy a ride-on lawnmower for a postage size lot. They have to call in a plumber for a leaky drain, when a bit of duct tape will solve the problem."

I watched him glance out the bay window at our tiny vegetable garden.

"And they buy a fancy scarecrow from the hardware store when a Halloween Mask and a broken hockey stick will work just as well."

We had learned much in our four years about how things are done in La Peñita de Jaltemba, Nayarit, Mexico.

We had learned how to make lounge cushions.

We had found the secret to using the unique cement laundry tubs. For some unknown reason, they have two sides: one has a deep bowl and the tap and the other has the drain. But a cut-off Coke bottle duct taped to the faucet will allow you to drain the deep side without having to scoop out all the water every once in a while.

We had even finally learned how to fix the odd virus growing in our wall which, much to our disappointment, never did take on the shape of something useful like the Virgin Mary, frustrating my plan to use it as a fundraiser.

We watched the locals snicker, as we slowly but steadily learned the Mexican way to do things. But it was born not of contempt or malice; it was instead tinged with puzzlement and a touch of pride. It said: "they are learning to be Mexicans."

But when the metal door to the apartment became so sticky that we had to push your shoulder into it to get it open, we knew we had a problem beyond our level of competence and we would have to call in an expert.

The old man from the metalworking shop just off the avenida studied the door carefully.

I pointed to the hinges and the lock and shrugged my shoulders.

"Malleta," was all he said.

Anne turned to me as we watched the red paint chips fly everywhere as he battered the metal door frame with the little hammer, swinging the door back and forth proudly to show us how it now opened freely.

"We're learning," I said.

"We may never become real locals," Anne replied, "but at least we've become Upper Canadian Mexicanos."

"And I will take that as a compliment."

EPILOGUE

Our fifth winter in La Peñita de Jaltemba, Mexico is coming to a close as I write these final words. I am sitting on a vacant lot with its view of the ocean obscured by fishing boats and a fisherman talking on his cell phone as he ogles the shapely Nord Americana in the silver and black bikini.

The plans for the malecon are now thirteen years old and gathering dust in a desk somewhere in Compostelo. But there are rumours anew. Construction will start next fall they say.

And it will surely happen one day. The march of condos and timeshares and new restaurants slowly but surely makes its way north from Puerto Vallarta. The beaches between Bucerias and Punta de Mita that were once a playground for folks from the working town of Mezcales are now accessible only to those with a million and a half to plunk down on a condo. Walmart has moved north to Mezcales and there is a Mega Store in Bucerias. And there will surely come a day when there will be a franchise from the Carlos and Charlie's chain that dominates every resort town in Mexico in Guayabitos and a Mega Store in La Peñita.

It will be a godsend for some. The landowners like our first landlords, Kenny and Laura, will be laughing all the way to the bank. And our Notario, Lic. Armando Manuel Ortega Gonzalez, will find lots of opportunities to shove great wads of cash into all his pockets. With construction booming, our friend Chuy will be able to trade in his rusted-out 1983 black Ford Pick-up and drive to the Home Depot in style, although I'm sure he will still see those 'Curva Peligrosa' signs as a great opportunity to pass. And Jesus who delivers the mail might get an upgrade from bicycle to scooter. Restaurants will flourish and the future will provide all kinds of options for Francisco Padilla, the first prince at the Spring Festival at Kinder Miguel Hildago.

But the fisherman will be pushed back even farther from their livelihood as the price of beachfront property soars. The supermercados and local butcher shops will no longer be able to compete. The B-B-Barrys of La Peñita will have to find a new cheap town with less gringos and fewer policia to call home. Traditions will be lost and the hand-woven baskets made by the Tarahumara Indians from the Copper Canyon will be for sale at the La Peñita market every Thursday.

La Peñita has changed much in the five winters that we have been coming here. And it has also changed me. In the ten years between our first bus ride to 'Why a Bee Toes' and my retirement, I often dreamed on how I would spend my golden years. I imagined golf and walks on the beach and day trips to small towns along the coast. And sometimes, I even thought it might be fun to help teach English to some school kids, without the stickers. But a winter of going to meetings and taking minutes and drafting press releases and operational procedures was certainly never on the radar screen.

But the town gets in your blood. Or, more precisely, the people of the town get in your blood. I will never forget our first day back in town for our second winter when Roberto the butcher and Sergio the Postmaster and the gentleman who runs the Internet Café, whose name I am ashamed to admit that I hadn't learned, all came out to warmly greet us, to shake our hands and to welcome us back to town. Or the look in the eyes of the children when Los Amigos de La Peñita helped to turn an over-grown rock-strewn field into a safe place for them to play. Or the cheerful 'holas' and 'buenos dias' that you get from people on the street, Mexicanos and gringos alike. Or the Nord Americanos who come out for the horseshoe tournament to raise money for scholarships and help teach English in the schools and worked with the locals to get a new home built for three kids orphaned by a car accident.

It's hard not to want to do your own small part to help make life just a little easier for the people in this tiny part of the world.

There are certain images that usually come to mind when you think about traveling to Mexico: five star resorts on glittering beaches, or, more recently, the gruesome carnage of the drug wars that litters the border with the United States.

But I hope that this book will create a different set of pictures in your mind:

- the owners of a bar having to restore the power line that the beer truck tore down before they serve you dinner and then drive you home;

- a Walmart bakery with six rows of nothing but Rosca de Reyes;

- two workers in the office of the old Santa Ana Hotel digging a well through the floor;

- the future mayor of the town of Los Ayala with a car sticker proudly plastered on his forehead;

- two street dogs playing an energetic game of 'Diaper Tag' on the beach;

- the first prince at the Spring Festival at Kinder Miguel Hildago dragging his mother down the street to get ice cream;

- and a vacant lot where I sit as I write these final words, a vacant lot, that many hope will stay that way for many years to come, the lot where they tore down the Russell Hotel.

ABOUT THE AUTHOR

<u>They Tore Down the Russell Hotel</u> is the first book by Dave Easby. Dave spends his summers in Ontario, Canada and his winters in La Peñita de Jaltemba, Nayarit, Mexico with his wife Anne and his Mexican rescue dog Amarillo. He retired in 2005 after a thirty year career with the Canadian and New Brunswick Governments. Since much of that time was spent working on speeches and briefing notes for Ministers and other Senior Officials, he decided to try writing non-fiction for a change in his retirement years.